The Official
Rails-to-Trails
Conservancy
Guidebook

Rail-Trails
West

Rail-Trails: West

1st EDITION 2009

Copyright © 2009 by Rails-to-Trails Conservancy

Cover photographs copyright © 2009 by Bryce Hall (main and inset right) and Rails-to-Trails Conservancy (inset left and back cover) All interior photographs by Rails-to-Trails Conservancy, except for the ones on pages 59 (inset) and 119, Boyd Loving; and 99, Darrin Gardiner.

Maps: Tim Rosner and Lohnes+Wright
Cover design: Lisa Pletka
Book design and layout: Lisa Pletka and Larry B. Van Dyke
Book editors: Laura Shauger, Jennifer Kaleba and Wendy Jordan

ISBN 978-0-89997-489-7

Manufactured in the United States of America

Published by: **Wilderness Press**
                   1345 8th Street
                   Berkeley, CA 94710
                   (800) 443-7227; FAX (510) 558-1696
                   info@wildernesspress.com
                   www.wildernesspress.com

Visit our website for a complete listing of our books and for ordering information.

Cover photos: Monterey Peninsula Recreational Trail *(main)*; Martin Luther King Promenade *(inset top)*; Lands End Trail *(inset bottom)*; Half Moon Bay Coastside Trail *(back cover)*

Title page photo: Delta Meadows River Park

SAFETY NOTICE: Although Wilderness Press and Rails-to-Trails Conservancy have made every attempt to ensure that the information in this book is accurate at press time, they are not responsible for any loss, damage, injury, or inconvenience that may occur to anyone while using this book. You are responsible for your own safety and health while in the wilderness. The fact that a trail is described in this book does not mean that it will be safe for you. Be aware that trail conditions can change from day to day. Always check local conditions, know your own limitations, and consult a map.

About Rails-to-Trails Conservancy

Headquartered in Washington, D.C., Rails-to-Trails Conservancy (RTC) fosters one great mission: to protect America's irreplaceable rail corridors by transforming them into multiuse trails. Its hope is that these pathways will reconnect Americans with their neighbors, communities, nature, and proud history.

Railways helped build America. Spanning from coast to coast, these ribbons of steel linked people, communities, and enterprises, spurring commerce and forging a single nation that bridges a continent. But in recent decades, many of these routes have fallen into disuse, severing communal ties that helped bind Americans together.

When RTC opened its doors in 1986, the rail-trail movement was in its infancy. While there were some 250 miles of open rail-trails in the United States, most projects focused on single, linear routes in rural areas, created for recreation and conservation. RTC sought broader protection for the unused corridors, incorporating rural, suburban, and urban routes.

Year after year, RTC's efforts to protect and align public funding with trail building created an environment that allowed trail advocates in communities all across the country to initiate trail projects. These ever-growing ranks of trail professionals, volunteers, and RTC supporters have built momentum for the national rail-trails movement. As the number of supporters multiplied, so too did the rail-trails. By the turn of the 21st century, there were some 1100 rail-trails on the ground, and RTC recorded nearly 84,000 supporters, from business leaders and politicians to environmentalists and healthy-living advocates.

Americans now enjoy more than 15,000 miles of open rail-trails. And as they flock to the trails to commune with neighbors, neighborhoods, and nature, their economic, physical, and environmental wellness continue to flourish.

In 2006, Rails-to-Trails Conservancy celebrated 20 years of creating, protecting, serving, and connecting rail-trails. Boasting more than 100,000 members and supporters, RTC is the nation's leading advocate for trails and greenways.

People use California's 4.4-mile Fairfield Linear Park to access Solano Community College Campus and the Fairfield city center.

Foreword

Dear Reader:

For those of you who have already experienced the sheer enjoyment and freedom of riding on a rail-trail, welcome back! You'll find *Rail-Trails: West* to be a useful and fun guide to your favorite trails, as well as an introduction to pathways you have yet to travel.

For readers who are discovering, for the first time, the adventures you can have on a rail-trail, thank you for joining the rail-trail movement. Since 1986, Rails-to-Trails Conservancy has been the No. 1 supporter and defender of these priceless public corridors. We are excited to bring you *Rail-Trails: West* so you, too, can enjoy this region's rail-trails.

Built on unused, former railroad corridors, these hiking and biking trails are an ideal way to connect with your community, with nature, and with your friends and family. I've found that rail-trails have a way of bringing people together, and as you'll see from this book, there are opportunities in every state you visit to get on a trail. Whether you're looking for a place to exercise, explore, commute, or play—there is a rail-trail in this book for you.

So I invite you to sit back, relax, pick a trail that piques your interest—and then get out, get active, and have some fun. I'll be out on the trails, too, so be sure to wave as you go by.

Happy Trails,

Keith Laughlin
President, Rails-to-Trails Conservancy

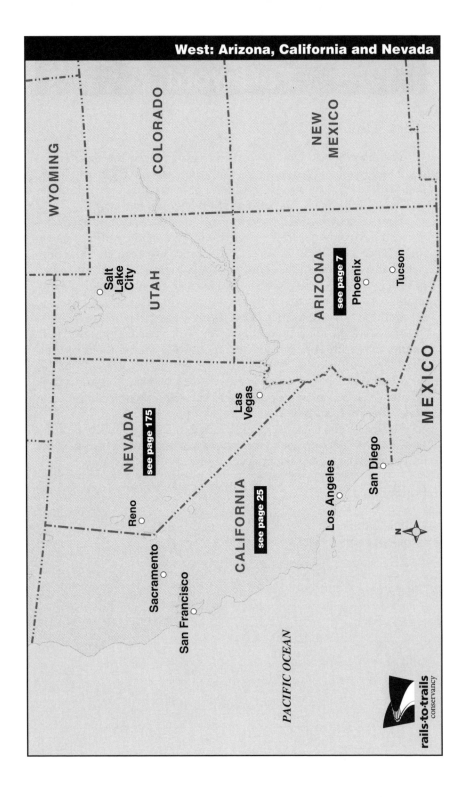

WYOMING

COLORADO

NEW MEXICO

Salt Lake City

UTAH

ARIZONA
see page 7
Phoenix

Tucson

NEVADA
see page 175

Las Vegas

MEXICO

Reno

San Diego

Los Angeles

CALIFORNIA
see page 25

Sacramento

San Francisco

PACIFIC OCEAN

N

rails-to-trails
conservancy

Contents

ARIZONA   7

CALIFORNIA   25

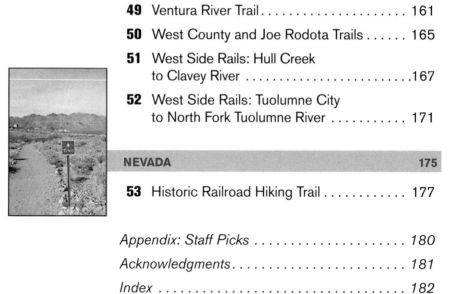

Fogged in or clear as a bell, the view from the peak of San Francisco's Lands End Trail is an unforgettable and unique rail-trail experience.

INTRODUCTION

Of the roughly 1,400 rail-trails across the U.S., *Rail-Trails: West* highlights 53 in Arizona, California and Nevada. These rail-trails tread storied routes of westward expansion and industrialization. They bear the signatures of their history, left behind in tunnels and trestles, raised berms and depots, communities born and abandoned.

Some of the original railroads in western states bridged vast stretches of forbidding desert and tied distant states together. Others fed gold mines and gold rushes, or served as logging lines through the pine canyons of northern California. Dozens more retrace the tracks of passenger and freight lines up and down the Pacific coast. Their original purposes and destinations vary, but each of these rail-trails joins past with present, creating a living memorial of the corridors that helped shape the West.

Many of Arizona's rail-trails showcase a sweeping desert landscape of sunbaked prairies and wind-worn mountains. Among the state's standout trails are the Peavine and Iron King in Prescott, where wildflowers cling to crevasses in boulders the size of buildings. Offering an even more rustic desert adventure, the Mohave and Milltown Railroad Trail follows a line that connected a gold mine with the Colorado River in 1903.

California's rail-trails anchor the West region and offer as diverse a geographic canvas as any state in the country. The Bayshore Bikeway in San Diego spins around tidal flats, salt marshes and bird sanctuaries along the Pacific Flyway. A little farther north, the San Clemente Pedestrian Beach Trail cruises between coastal bluffs and a shoreline of sand dunes and sea breezes. Other popular trails in northern California, like the Bizz Johnson National Recreation Trail from Susanville to Mason Station, tour weaving canyons, rushing creeks and mountainscapes. Yet you'll find some of the most dramatic views on urban pathways, like the Lands End Trail in San Francisco, where the Golden Gate Bridge crowns the horizon.

Nevada has only one rail-trail featured in *Rail-Trails: West*, but it's as rich in history as it is in stunning landscapes. The Historic Railroad Hiking Trail snakes through five railroad tunnels along tracks once used to build the Hoover Dam in the 1930s. What the state lacks in rail-trail numbers, this pathway more than makes up for with its backdrop of Lake Mead, the Colorado River and a gnarled, volcanic landscape.

Whichever route you choose to explore, you'll get a ground-level taste of the expansive West—its sparkling shorelines, lonesome canyons and mountain ranges, and the railroads that once connected them.

What is a Rail-Trail?

Rail-trails are multiuse public paths built along former railroad corridors. Most often flat or following a gentle grade, they are suited to walking, running, cycling, mountain biking, inline skating, cross-country skiing, horseback riding, and wheelchair use. Since the 1960s, Americans have created more than 15,000 miles of rail-trails throughout the country.

These extremely popular recreation and transportation corridors traverse urban, suburban, and rural landscapes. Many preserve historic landmarks, while others serve as wildlife conservation corridors, linking isolated parks and establishing greenways in developed areas. Rail-trails also stimulate local economies by boosting tourism and promoting trailside businesses.

What is a Rail-with-Trail?

A rail-with-trail is a public path that parallels a still-active rail line. Some run adjacent to high-speed, scheduled trains, often linking public transportation stations, while others follow tourist routes and slow-moving excursion trains. Many share an easement, separated from the rails by extensive fencing. There are more than 115 rails-with-trails in the U.S.

HOW TO USE THIS BOOK

*R*ail-Trails: West provides the information you need to plan a rewarding rail-trail trek. With words to inspire you and maps to chart your path, it makes choosing the best route a breeze. Following are some of the highlights.

Maps

You'll find three levels of maps in this book: an **overall regional map**, **state locator maps**, and **detailed trail maps**.

The western region includes California, Nevada, and Arizona. Each chapter details a particular state's network of trails, marked on locator maps in the chapter introduction. Use these maps to find the trails nearest you, or select several neighboring trails and plan a weekend hiking or biking excursion. Once you find a trail on a state locator map, simply flip to the corresponding page number for a full description. Accompanying trail maps mark each route's access roads, trailheads, parking areas, restrooms, and other defining features.

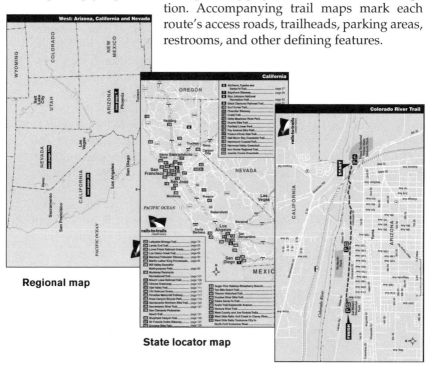

Regional map

State locator map

Trail map

3

Trail Descriptions

Trails are listed in alphabetical order within each chapter. Each description leads off with a set of summary information, including trail endpoints and mileage, a roughness index, the trail surface, and possible uses.

The map and summary information list the trail endpoints (either a city, street, or more specific location), with suggested points from which to start and finish. Additional access points are marked on the maps and mentioned in the trail descriptions. The maps and descriptions also highlight available amenities, including parking and restrooms, as well as such area attractions as shops, services, museums, parks, and stadiums. Trail length is listed in miles.

Each trail bears a roughness index rating from 1 to 3. A rating of 1 indicates a smooth, level surface that is accessible to users of all ages and abilities. A 2 rating means the surface may be loose and/or uneven and could pose a problem for road bikes and wheelchairs. A 3 rating suggests a rough surface that is only recommended for mountain bikers and hikers. Surfaces can range from asphalt or concrete to ballast, cinder, crushed stone, gravel, grass, dirt, and/or sand. Where relevant, trail descriptions address alternating surface conditions.

All rail-trails are open to pedestrians, and most allow bicycles, except where noted in the trail summary or description. The summary also indicates wheelchair access. Other possible uses include inline skating, mountain biking, hiking, horseback riding, fishing, and cross-country skiing. While most trails are off-limits to motor vehicles, some local trail organizations do allow ATVs and snowmobiles.

Trail descriptions themselves suggest an ideal itinerary for each route, including the best parking areas and access points, where to begin, your direction of travel, and any highlights along the way. The text notes any connecting or neighboring routes, with page numbers for the respective trail descriptions. Following each description are directions to the recommended trailheads.

Each trail description also lists a local contact (name, address, phone number, and website) for further information. Be sure to call these trail managers or volunteer groups in advance for updates and current conditions.

Key to Map Icons

Parking

Drinking water

Bathrooms

Trail Use

Rail-trails are popular routes for a range of uses, often making them busy places to play. Trail etiquette applies. If passing other trail users on your bicycle, always try to pass on the left with an audible warning such as a bike-mounted bell or a polite but firm, "Passing on your left!" For your safety and that of other trail users, keep children and pets from straying into oncoming trail traffic. Keep dogs leashed, and supervise children until they can demonstrate proper behavior.

Cyclists and inline skaters should wear helmets, reflective clothing, and other safety gear, as some trails involve hazardous road crossings. It's also best to bring a flashlight or bike- or helmet-mounted light for tunnel passages or twilight excursions.

Key to Trail Use

walking	hiking	cycling	mountain biking	inline skating

fishing	horseback riding	cross-country skiing	snowmobile	wheelchair access

Learn More

While *Rail-Trails: West* is a helpful guide to available routes in the region, it wasn't feasible to list every rail-trail in California, Arizona, and Nevada, and new rail-trails spring up each year. To learn about additional rail-trails in your area or to plan a trip to an area beyond the scope of this book, log on to the Rails-to-Trails Conservancy home page (www.railstotrails.org) and click on the Find a Trail link. RTC's online database lists more than 1400 rail-trails nationwide, searchable by state, county, city, trail name, surface type, length, activity, and/or keywords regarding your interest. A number of listings include photos and reviews from people who've already visited the trail.

Arizona

UTAH

NEVADA

St George   89

93

Page

15

160

Las
Vegas

89

93

Kingman

3

40

40

Prescott

4

93

Lake
Havasu
City

60

10

5

2 Flagstaff

Holbrook   180

17

ARIZONA

60

PHOENIX

191

70

NEW MEXICO

CALIFORNIA

1

8

Yuma

85

Casa
Grande

10

TUCSON   10

86

19

rails·to·trails
conservancy

M E X I C O

Arizona

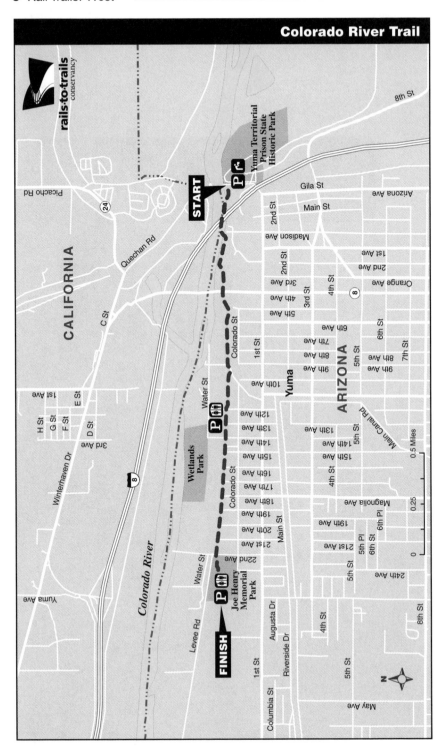

Colorado River Trail

Colorado River Trail

Experience the historic desert Southwest by visiting the Colorado River Trail in Yuma, Ariz. This pleasant trail along the banks of the Colorado River provides scenic vistas reminiscent of old western films. Located in the southwestern corner of Arizona, on the Mexico border, Yuma has one of the warmest climates in the country, making this trail perfect for a winter getaway.

Yuma was a central transportation hub in the late 1800s and early 1900s. Particularly because the railroad bridge crossed the Colorado River at its easiest point, Yuma became a major stop on the route to California. Yuma was also home to one of the most infamous correctional facilities of the Old West, the Yuma Territorial Prison. The town is a wonderful place to explore western heritage, and the Colorado River Trail is a great place to start.

The Colorado River Trail melds past with present—an early 1900s railroad hub turned rail-trail enjoyed by the whole community.

Location
Yuma County

Endpoints
North San Francisco Street and Route 66 to North Fanning Drive and Route 66

Mileage
1.5

Roughness Index
1

Surface
Asphalt

The trail skirts the edge of town on the abandoned Yuma Valley Railroad corridor near the banks of the Colorado River. Begin at the Yuma Territorial Prison State Historical Park near the Fourth Avenue Bridge. Along the river, the park features picnic tables, restrooms and a riverfront beach. From here the trail heads west along the unused tracks.

This 1.5-mile paved trail is an enjoyable smooth journey. The trail is also commonly refered to as the Yuma Crossing Bike Path. About halfway along the trail, you will see a connection to the East Main Canal Bike Path on your left that takes you along the Main Canal to the southern end of town.

As you travel along the path you are treated to breathtaking views of the surrounding mountains. And, even though this is a desert region, the Colorado River feeds farms in the valley. The trail ends at Joe Henry Memorial Park, a grassy park equipped with restrooms, picnic areas and ball fields.

DIRECTIONS

To reach the eastern trailhead, take the Winterhaven Drive/4th Avenue exit from Interstate 8 and turn south (right or left, depending on the direction you came from). After a half mile take a left onto 1st Street. Go 0.3 mile and take a left onto North Madison Avenue. Go one block, then take a right onto North Gila Street. The trailhead is on the left just a few hundred feet ahead.

To reach the western trailhead, take the Winterhaven Drive/4th Avenue exit from I-8 and turn south (right or left, depending on the direction you came from). After a half mile take a right onto 1st Street. Go 1.3 miles and turn right onto North 22nd Avenue. Go one block and take a left onto Colorado Street. The trailhead is on the right in Joe Henry Memorial Park, which has baseball fields.

Contact: City of Yuma Parks and Recreation
One City Plaza
P.O. Box 13012
Yuma, AZ 85366
(928) 373-5243
www.ci.yuma.az.us/1357.htm

Fort Tuthill Trail

Internationally renowned for outdoor recreation activities and as the launching point for visits to Grand Canyon National Park, Flagstaff also boasts one of the best community trail systems (known as the Flagstaff Urban Trails System) in the state. The Fort Tuthill Trail is an integral part of the system. One of many beautiful recreational trails in the area, this crushed stone rail-trail doubles as a commuter route for people who live on the south side of Flagstaff.

The quintessential western mountain town, Flagstaff offers a wide variety of activities, including hiking, skiing, camping, rock climbing and rafting. It is also home to the University of Northern Arizona and blends a youthful vibe with the spirit of the Old West.

The trail begins about 3 miles south of town at Ft. Tuthill County Park, a large park and campground and site of the Coconino County Fairgrounds. From here, the trail flows north through a high pinyon pine forest. The

The Fort Tuthill Trail is part of the Flagstaff Urban Trail System, a popular trail network running throughout the region.

Location
Coconino County

Endpoints
Fort Tuthill to
University Heights

Mileage
3

**Roughness
Index**
1

Surface
Crushed stone

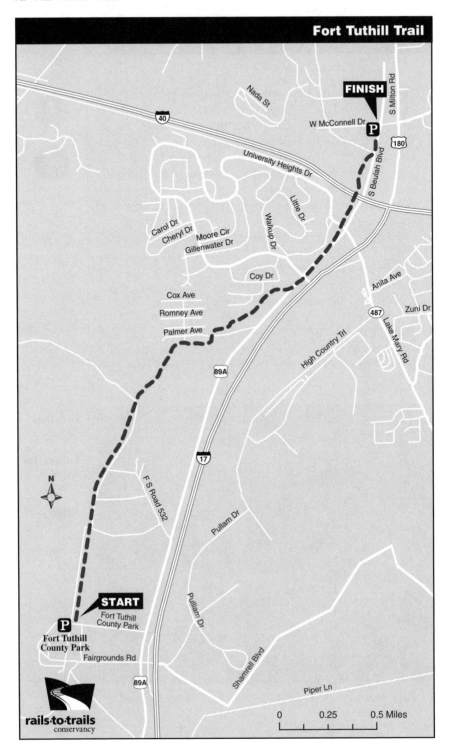

magnificent, snowcapped Humphreys Peak—at 12,633 feet Arizona's highest peak—looms in the distance.

After the first mile the setting changes from forest to a quiet residential area. Many locals hop on the trail here to commute downtown. Once past the neighborhood the corridor becomes wild again. After passing through the neighborhood, you reach Beulah Boulevard. The trail follows this busy road as it crosses underneath Interstate 40. When it reaches a bike and pedestrian bridge just beyond the interstate, the trail leaves the road and crosses a small creek.

Once you cross the creek you enter a busy commercial area called University Heights. A large shopping center that you will see on the left includes a number of restaurants and shops. The trail officially ends at the intersection of South Beulah Boulevard and West McConnell Drive. To continue to downtown Flagstaff, follow a connecting trail that leads off to the right and is part of the Flagstaff Urban Trails System.

DIRECTIONS

To reach the southern trailhead, take the Fairgrounds Road exit from Interstate 17 and go west (right or left, depending on the direction you came from). Take an immediate right onto Highway 89A. After just under 0.2 mile turn left into Ft. Tuthill County Park, and park in the lot. The trailhead is in the wooded area near the track.

To reach the northern trailhead, West McConnell Drive trailhead, take the South Milton Road north exit from the I-17 and I-40 interchange. Take an immediate left onto West McConnell Drive. Go 0.2 mile, cross South Beulah Boulevard, and reach the shopping area parking lot, where you will find the trail in the northeast corner.

Contact: Coconino County Parks and Recreation
HC 39 Box 3A
Fort Tuthill County Park
Flagstaff, AZ 86001
(928) 679-8000
www.coconino.az.gov/parks.aspx?id=408

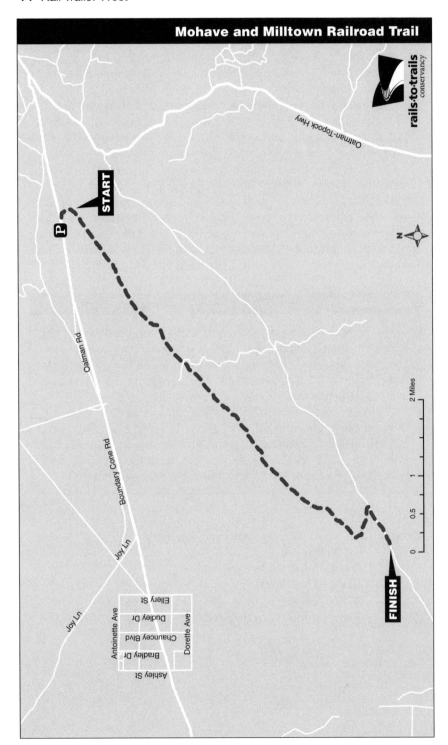

Mohave and Milltown Railroad Trail

Mohave and Milltown Railroad Trail

For a challenging desert adventure, travel the Mohave and Milltown Railroad Trail in northwest Arizona. The trail occupies the corridor of the historic Mohave and Milltown Railroad, a private narrow gauge railroad built in 1903 that connected a gold mine near Oatman, Ariz., with the Colorado River. Due to washouts in the desert, the railroad was in operation for only one year, and the corridor became inactive in 1904. The trail follows the railroad bed through a remote region of Mohave County, surrounded by desert mountains and plateaus.

This rail-trail is suitable only for advanced mountain bikers and hikers, as the surface is rough ballast. A path for off-road vehicles and equestrians parallels and frequently crosses the railroad bed. The best time to travel the trail is September through May. The Bureau of Land Management, which maintains the trail, recommends using caution when visiting the Mohave and Milltown

Location
Mohave County

Endpoints
Harpers Wash Road
to Boundary Cone
Road/Oatman Road

Mileage
7

**Roughness
Index**
1

Surface
Ballast

Rugged as the surrounding terrain, the Mohave and Milltown Railroad Trail is an atypical but rewarding rail-trail.

Railroad Trail in the summer months because the average temperature exceeds 100°F.

Pick up the trail at the eastern trailhead, off of Boundary Cone Road, where you'll find a small parking area and a trail sign. Near the sign is a narrow single-track path leading away from the parking lot. Follow this for about 0.25 mile to the old railroad grade.

From here the trail takes you west, following a slight decline for its entire length. Detours are sometimes necessary where the grade has washed away from flooding. Signs, directional indicators and rock cairns along the way keep you on course

Down in the Colorado River Valley below, brilliant green pastures provide a sense of life in this stunningly desolate landscape. If there is a lot of winter rain, you'll also find abundant wildflowers from February through April.

The trail ends at a Bureau of Land Management road. The trailhead is not as defined as the one at Boundary Cone Road, but you will recognize the road because there is nothing else around but desert sage.

If you have extra time, be sure to make a trip to Oatman, which is only about 5 miles from the Boundary Cone Road trailhead on historic Route 66. This gem of the Old West will take you back in time about a century and has a wide selection of restaurants, shops and tourist attractions.

DIRECTIONS

To reach the Boundary Cone Road trailhead, from Interstate 40 in Needles, Calif., take the J Street exit going east. After 0.2 mile take a left on Front Street. Go one block to K Street and take a right. K Street becomes SR 95 here. Follow SR 95 for 8.9 miles, then take a right onto Boundary Cone Road. The trailhead and parking are 9.2 miles ahead on the right side of the road.

Contact: Arizona Bureau of Land Management
Kingman Field Office
2755 Mission Boulevard
Kingman, AZ 86401
(928) 718-3700
www.blm.gov/az/st/en/prog/recreation/hiking/mohave_
milltown_rr.print.html

Peavine and Iron King Trails

To say that the connected rail-trails of Prescott are oases in sun-baked, north-central Arizona is no exaggeration. Wherever water touches this arid landscape—and it does along the Peavine and Iron King trails—jade cottonwoods cluster, popping out against the desert's pale yellow and burnt brown pallet. And, at 5,300 feet above sea level, with cool breezes tempered by hot sunshine, Prescott is an ideal place for trail trips in the late winter and spring.

The 4-mile Peavine Trail begins just south of Watson Lake at the gravel parking lot by the lush Watson Woods Riparian Preserve. The crushed stone and dirt trail runs through a sea of green as it traverses the preserve. Through the trees you may even hear the rush of nearby Granite Creek, swollen after a bout of rain.

A mile in, the trail leaves the preserve and curves around the southern end of Lake Watson to reach the Granite Dells, massive mounds of weather-beaten rock.

Location
Yavapai County

Endpoints
South of Highway 89A to north of Prescott Lakes Parkway

Iron King and Peavine Trail junction to North Glassford Hill Road

Mileage
4 (Peavine)
3 (Iron King)

Roughness Index
2

Surface
Dirt, crushed stone, ballast, cinder

A view of Lake Watson and the Granite Dells from the Peavine Trail

17

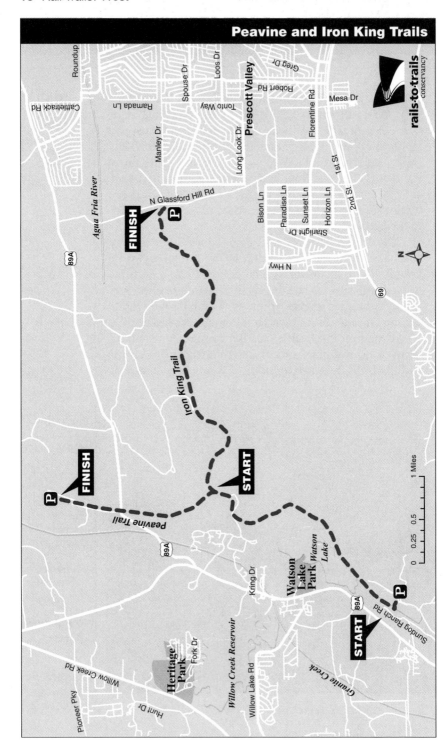

Peavine and Iron King Trails

rails-to-trails
conservancy

This natural formation is a big tourist draw, and you'll see the majority of fellow trail users here. It's no wonder: As you pass through the cool cuts in the granite, you're enfolded in a kind of castle of desert stone.

All along this route, water leaches from cracks in the rock walls and improbable, hearty flowers—red and yellow—pop from the crevasses. The temptation to scramble up the smooth, stony inclines for a scenic vista is keen, but no sight is more arresting than the perfectly framed view of far-off Granite Mountain over Lake Watson.

Once you've pulled your eyes and your camera away from the view, continue heading northward. The trail follows the former Santa Fe, Prescott & Phoenix Railway corridor that fed into Prescott, once the territorial capital of Arizona and famous for its copper mining. Wooden decking and railroad ties lie scattered along the trail. At mile 3 and the "Point of Rocks," the railroad's ghost is impossible to miss. Here the trail passes through a cut made for trains in a tall, sheer rock cluster. A trailside historical marker shows a photo of the identical view, taken some 100 years earlier. In the photo a hulking engine chugs through the pass.

Beyond Point of Rocks, you reach a fork in the trail. Head left to continue on the Peavine for 1 mile to its endpoint atop a gravel-covered railroad bridge. A two-lane country road runs beneath you, and private property spreads in vast tracts beyond. As tantalizing as the call of the open range might be, don't consider trespassing. Instead, head back to that fork in the road, turn right, and hop on the 3-mile Iron King Trail.

The Dells dwarfed you with their massiveness, but the Iron King makes you feel small in a different way. On this trail you are engulfed in scraggly desert woods. A fenced-in bull grazes near a lonely pond and grunts as you pass. Off-shooting trails disappear in the underbrush, and every mile or so a haunting railroad relic stands guard. Rusted, gutted, but plainly beautiful old train cars (smaller than most) are mounted at intervals along the trail. They're striking in their isolation, especially against the pale desert backdrop. As the Iron King breaks free of the forest and rolls into an expanse of prairie, the vistas on this stretch are impressive in an entirely opposite way from The Dells—the land simply lays itself bare. Low, cream-tinted hills, bent prairie grasses and a haze of dust reach out toward distant mountain ranges as the trail ambles slightly downhill. A tumbleweed rolls by, so perfectly placed you look around for the Hollywood prop master.

In the distance, the town of Prescott Valley comes into view. About a mile before trail's end (and the miles stretch out deceptively on this trail) the railroad corridor merges into an extra-wide dirt trail to reach North Glassford Hill Road and Iron King's somewhat unspectacular finish. But no worries—you have all that stunning trail behind you and nothing but time to soak it in.

DIRECTIONS

To reach the Peavine and Iron King trails trailhead, head north on Interstate 17, exit onto Highway 69 North at Cordes Junction. Instead of going into downtown Prescott, turn right onto 89 North toward Chino Valley. After 2 miles, turn right onto Prescott Lakes Parkway. Follow Prescott Lakes Parkway across Granite Creek. Turn left onto Sundog Ranch Road. A sign for the rail-trail marks your left turn into the parking lot for both the Peavine Trail and the Watson Woods Riparian Preserve.

Contact: Flagstaff Parks and Recreation Department
211 West Aspen Avenue
Flagstaff, AZ 86001
(928) 770-7690
http://flagstaff.az.gov/index.asp?nid=11

Route 66 Trail

The Route 66 Trail in Flagstaff begins in the heart of the beautiful historic downtown district right next to the picturesque Flagstaff Train Depot. Parking is available right along historic Route 66 at the visitor center adjacent to the trailhead. The trail runs between Route 66 and the active railroad tracks that are a defining feature of this mountain town.

Spend just a small amount of time in Flagstaff and the unmistakable whistle of a train engine pierces the air multiple times every hour. This town is not a relic of past railroading glories; the trains and the timber industry that helped settle the area are still a vital and visible part of the community.

Leaving the downtown area the concrete trail stays adjacent to the roadway, meandering just a few feet off the road's edge at times. The active railroad tracks are rarely more than a hundred feet to the south. A multitude of shopping plazas, restaurants and lodging

Paralleling the famed Route 66, the trail connects Flagstaff shops, neighborhoods and restaurants.

Location
Coconino County

Endpoints
San Francisco Street to North Fanning Drive

Mileage
3.6

Roughness Index
1

Surface
Concrete

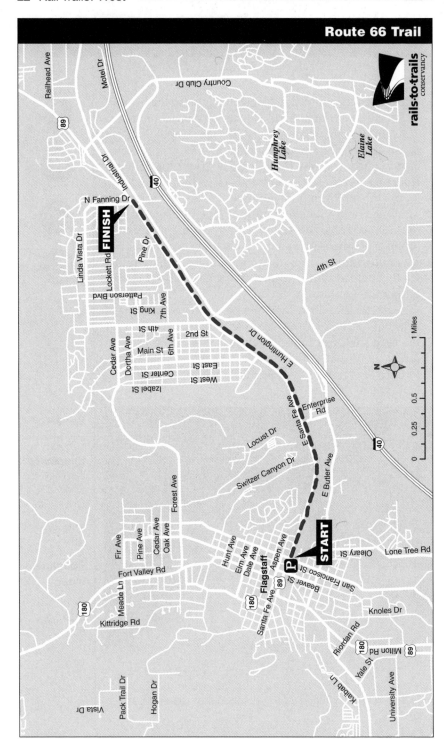

Route 66 Trail

accommodations dominate the opposite side of the road for the majority of this trail. No matter how much traffic goes by, both car and train, it is impossible to not sneak a peek to the north and enjoy the pristine views of the San Francisco Peaks and the towering pines that cover their slopes. At about mile 1.1 you use the crosswalk to negotiate Enterprise Road, one of only two road crossings that force a stop on the trail.

After the road crossing, the trail and road take a significant turn to the north and enter a distinctly different part of town. The increase in locals out on the trail—walking, biking and even carrying groceries—signifies that this part of town has more of a residential component to it. The second road crossing at North Steves Boulevard is at mile 2.8 and leaves less than a mile to the trail's current endpoint. The final straight stretch goes by quickly. Look for the shopping plaza on the left just before the trail ends at North Fanning Drive; this is the parking area for this end of the trail.

DIRECTIONS

To reach the downtown trailhead from Interstate 17, take South Milton Road (Route 89) north for 1.9 miles. Take a right onto Route 66. The trailhead is on the right in 0.3 mile, at the corner of San Francisco Street. Parking is available at the visitor center on Route 66.

To reach the eastern trailhead from I-17, take Highway 180/89 North. Cross the overpass and follow the signs for Flagstaff. After 0.75 mile, Route 89 becomes Route 66. At this convergence the trailhead is located on the corner of Route 66 and North Fanning Drive. Parking is available at the shopping plaza across Route 66.

Contact: Flagstaff Parks and Recreation Department
211 West Aspen Avenue
Flagstaff, AZ 86001
(928) 770-7690
http://flagstaff.az.gov/index.asp?nid=11

California

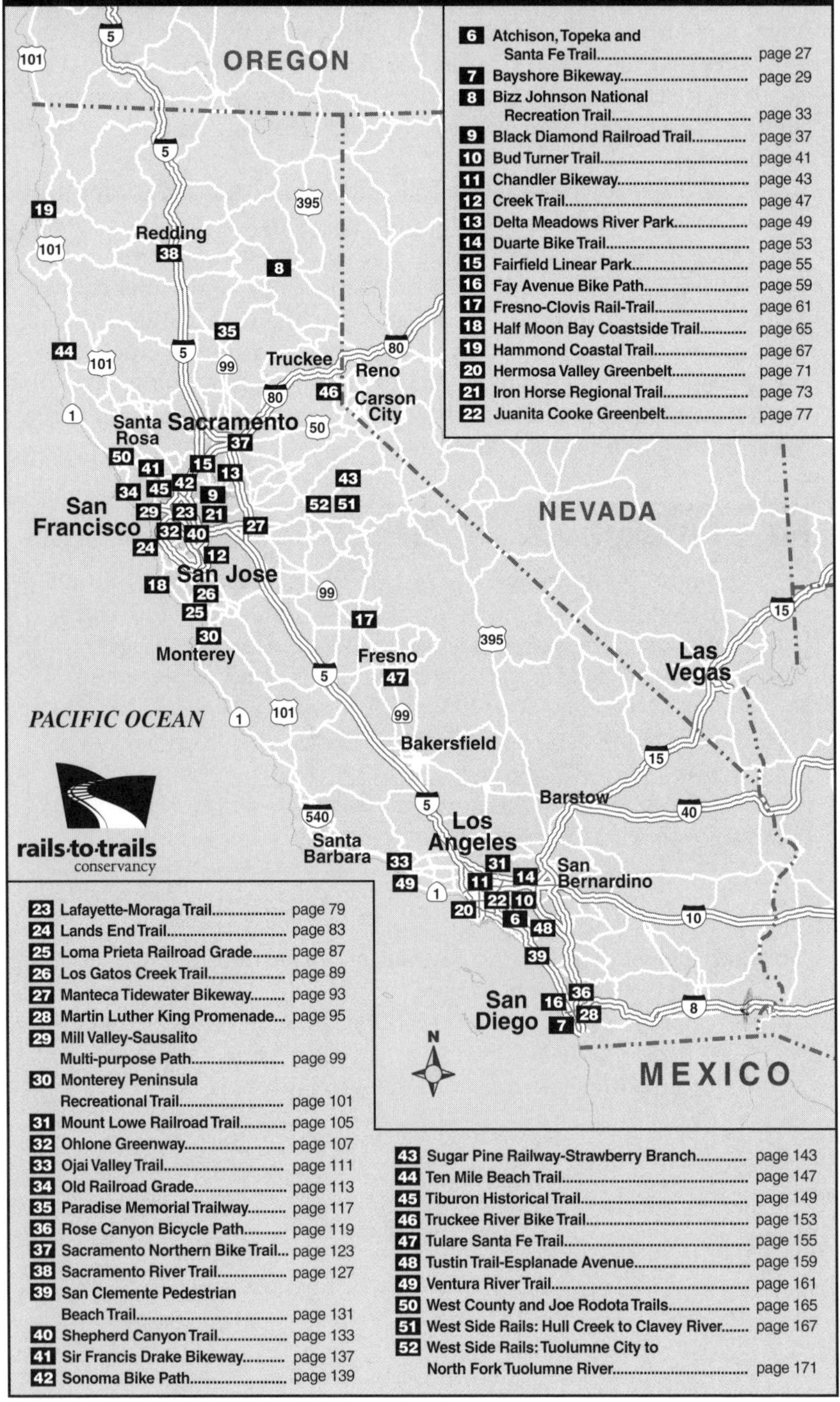

OREGON

NEVADA

Redding

Truckee
Reno
Carson City

Santa Rosa
Sacramento

San Francisco

San Jose

Monterey

PACIFIC OCEAN

Fresno

Bakersfield

rails·to·trails
conservancy

Barstow

Santa Barbara

Los Angeles
San Bernardino

Las Vegas

San Diego

MEXICO

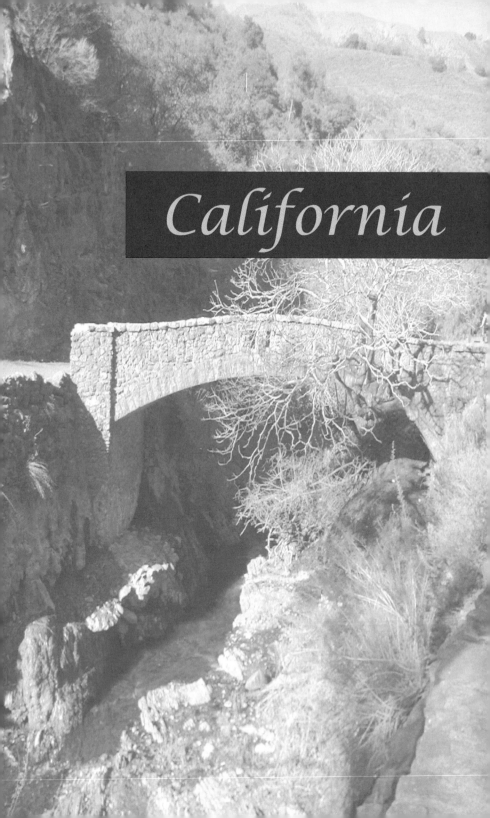

California

Atchison, Topeka and Santa Fe Trail

Michelle Dr

5

261

El Camino Real

Bryan Ave

Walnut Ave

Jamboree Rd

Hicks Canyon Community Park

Park Pl

Irvine Blvd

Culver Dr

Silkwood Park

Havard Square Park

Brywood Park

Colony Park

Yale Ave

FINISH

261

College Park

Walnut Ave

Coralwood Park

Heritage Park

Harvard Ave

Flagstone Park
Windwood Park

Orchard Park

5

Jeffrey Rd

Santa Luisa Park

Roosevelt

Santa Cruz Park

Hayes St

Trabuco Rd

Culver Dr

Deerfield Community Park

Irvine

Yale Ave

Birdsong Park

Ranch Park

North Lake Park

Marine Way

Woodbridge Community Park

University Dr

Chenile

Orangetree Park

START

5

405

Sand Canyon Ave

Irvine Center Dr

Pine Brook Park

Waterworks Way

Valley Oak Park

Dovecreek Park

Barranca Pky

Laguna Canyon Rd

Alton Pky

N

0   0.25   0.5   1 Miles

405

rails·to·trails
conservancy

Atchison, Topeka and Santa Fe Trail

This great trail shares a wide corridor with an active railroad line, a Burlington Northern Santa Fe route, through a section of Orange County known for producing oranges and strawberries.

The Atchison, Topeka and Santa Fe Railroad line originally provided a vital link for transporting iron from the Midwest into the Los Angeles area. In 1971, Amtrak assumed operation of the line, using it to transport passengers between Chicago and Los Angeles. Burlington Northern officially maintains the track and uses it for freight rail, in conjunction with the Amtrak and Metrolink passenger service.

The trail itself begins off Sand Canyon Avenue just south of the railroad tracks. This well-maintained and smooth-paved trail follows the tracks heading northwest. You will cut through a section of the lush Oak Creek Golf Club before reaching the intersection of Jeffrey Road. An underpass here provides safe, uninterrupted trail travel.

The Atchison, Topeka and Santa Fe Trail is a rail-with-trail, sharing its wide, smooth corridor with train service.

Beyond Jeffrey Road, the trail passes grassy Hoeptner Park, a nice spot to rest or have a picnic. From here the trail crosses some pleasant neighborhoods. There are access points all along the trail, making it a popular commuting route.

From here, the trail passes underneath Yale Avenue and continues to busy Culver Drive where a trail overpass carries you across the road. In addition, there are access points to the street and sidewalks if you need to connect to sections of town.

Location
Orange County

Endpoints
Sand Canyon Avenue to Harvard Avenue

Mileage
5

Roughness Index
1

Surface
Asphalt

The trail continues through Flagstone Park, which provides a nice rest spot before making the final push toward the end of the trail. At Harvard Avenue, the trail ends, but there are multiple connections here to bike lanes and other small trails to other parts of the city and region.

DIRECTIONS

To reach the Sand Canyon Avenue trailhead, take the Sand Canyon Avenue exit from Interstate 5. Go west on Sand Canyon Avenue for 0.5 mile, across the Orange County Transportation Authority (OCTA) Metrolink Railroad tracks. The trail is on the right (west) and is marked by a sign that reads WALNUT TRAIL. There is no parking at this endpoint, but you might find on-street parking along Oak Canyon Road, which is about 100 yards west of the trail.

To reach the Harvard Avenue endpoint, take the Culver Drive exit from Interstate 5. Take Culver Drive west for 0.5 mile to Walnut Ave. Turn right (north) on Walnut and go 0.5 mile to Harvard Avenue. Go left (west) on Harvard for 0.5 mile, crossing the OCTA Metrolink tracks, to the trail, which is marked here also with a WALNUT TRAIL sign. There is limited on-street parking here and on nearby neighborhood streets.

Contact: Orange County Transportation Authority
550 South Main Street
P.O. Box 14184
Orange, CA 92868
(714) 636-RIDE (7433)
www.octa.net

Bayshore Bikeway

C oastal rail-trail experiences don't get much better than this—a long, smooth palm-tree-lined trail with stunning views of the Pacific, San Diego Bay, and the downtown skyline, plus easy access to parks, tot play areas and chic cafes.

Before you start on the trail, please note that the coastal leg of the trail along this bikeway can be windy, especially in the afternoon. If you want the wind mostly at your back, ride the trail from north to south.

Paved portions of trail are wheelchair accessible, but a section of the trail near 10th Street and Glorietta Boulevard is an on-street bike lane and not a separate trail. Also, the route of the Bayshore Bikeway on the east side of the bay is predominantly on-street bike lanes.

The Bayshore (or Silver Strand) Bikeway sets out from Coronado Ferry Landing and the Ferry Landing Marketplace. Bring your bike over on the San Diego-Coronado Ferry (www.coronadoferrylandingshops.com/

Location
San Diego County

Endpoints
Coronado to Imperial Beach

Mileage
11

Roughness Index
1

Surface
Asphalt

A sleek, urban trail, the 11-mile Bayshore Bikeway is a pedal-push away from Pacific Ocean and San Diego Bay access, with plenty of amenities to spare.

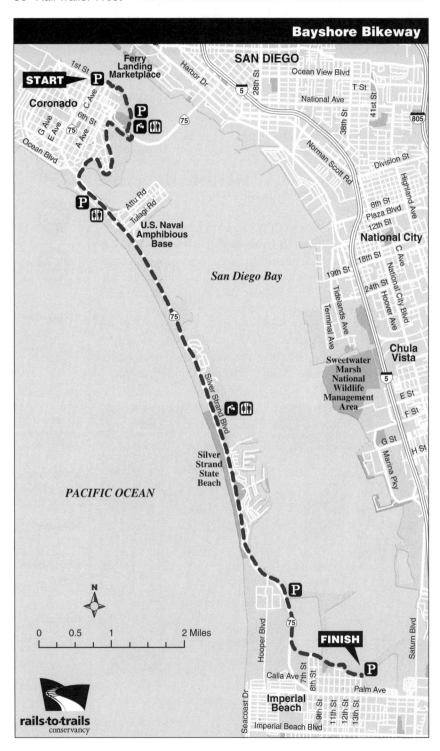

Bayshore Bikeway

SAN DIEGO

Ferry Landing Marketplace

Ocean View Blvd

1st St

START P

Coronado

G Ave
E Ave
A Ave
6th St
C Ave

75

Ocean Blvd

Harbor Dr

5

28th St

National Ave

T St

41st St

805

Norman Scott Rd

Division St

Highland Ave

Attu Rd

Tulagi Rd

P

U.S. Naval Amphibious Base

San Diego Bay

8th St
Plaza Blvd
12th St

National City

75

18th St

19th St

24th St

C Ave

National City Blvd

Hoover Ave

Tidelands Ave

Terminal Ave

Chula Vista

Sweetwater Marsh National Wildlife Management Area

5

E St

F St

Silver Strand Blvd

Silver Strand State Beach

G St

Marina Pky

H St

PACIFIC OCEAN

N

0   0.5   1   2 Miles

P

75

Hooper Blvd

FINISH

P

Saturn Blvd

Calla Ave

7th St
8th St

Palm Ave

rails·to·trails
conservancy

Seacoast Dr

Imperial Beach

9th St
11th St
12th St
13th St

Imperial Beach Blvd

san-diego-bay-ferry.htm), or rent one at the Bikes & Beyond shop. Head south along the path past some upscale restaurants and trailside cafes. You can take in wonderful views of the downtown San Diego skyline as you skirt Tidelands Park, with its grassy fields and playground.

Bike underneath the beautiful, arching Coronado Bridge and keep your head up as you roll past the Coronado Golf Course, a public course with million-dollar views. As you wind around the perimeter of the golf course, the separated bike path ends and you cross over to the right side of Glorietta Boulevard, into the on-road bike lane for a short distance. At 10th Street and Glorietta Boulevard, cross Glorietta and pick up the off-street path again. A sign marking the trail here says BAYSHORE BIKEWAY & IMPERIAL BEACH.

To your right you might recognize the signature red roof of the historic Hotel del Coronado. Marilyn Monroe fans may recognize the hotel, built in 1888, as the location for the Miami Beach scenes in *Some Like it Hot*.

Cutting south from the hotel, the pathway follows the Silver Strand, the narrow spit of land separating San Diego Bay and the Pacific Ocean where the Coronado branch of the San Diego and Arizona Eastern Railroad once traveled. The railroad was begun by prominent San Diego resident John D. Spreckels in 1906 and completed in 1919. It was constructed to link San Diego to the Southern Pacific Railroad in El Centro, Calif. In 1932, Spreckel's heirs sold their share of the railroad to Southern Pacific, and in 1933, it became the San Diego and Arizona Eastern Railway.

On the left is the Coronado Community Center and a beautiful bayside park that's perfect for an afternoon picnic. Following the narrow, blustery corridor with shorelines and sand dunes on both sides of the rail-trail, you'll pass the large U.S. Naval Amphibious Base (where Navy SEALs train), and then a half-mile nature path with observation decks and interpretive signs. At Silver Strand State Beach, pedestrian tunnels beneath Highway 75 offer access to the bigger surf on the ocean side, or the calmer, warmer waters on the bay side.

Beyond the state beach is the San Diego Bay National Wildlife Refuge, which was dedicated in June 1999 and contains the majority of the remaining wetlands, mudflats and eelgrass beds in San Diego Bay. The 3,940-acre refuge supports many endangered and threatened species of flora and fauna, which makes it an important stop on the Pacific Flyway, a north-south migratory bird route along the Americas. Visitors can bird watch from various points along the bike path.

The continuous, paved portion of the rail-trail ends at the south end of San Diego Bay in Imperial Beach. To complete the 24-mile loop around the bay, the rail-trail links with well-marked on-street bike lanes and bike routes through Chula Vista, National City and downtown San Diego and on to the San Diego-Coronado Ferry.

DIRECTIONS

To reach the Coronado trailhead by car, from downtown San Diego take Interstate 5 to the Highway 75 exit. Cross the San Diego-Coronado Bay Bridge and follow Highway 75, which becomes Fourth Street, to Orange Avenue. Turn right (east) onto First Street. A shopping center and the ferry terminal are just south of Orange Avenue and First Street. Park in the shopping center lot or on the street.

You can also reach the trailhed from downtown San Diego on the San Diego-Coronado Ferry, which runs all day and allows bikes. For schedule and fee information, visit www.coronadoferrylandingshops.com/san-diego-bay-ferry.htm.

To reach the Imperial Beach trailhead, from near the terminus of Interstate 5 in Chula Vista, take Highway 75/Palm Avenue east to 13th Street and turn right (north) to the trailhead parking lot.

Contact: San Diego Association of Governments (SANDAG)
401 B Street, Suite 800
San Diego, CA 92101
(619) 699-1924
www.sandag.org/bayshorebikeway

Bizz Johnson National Recreation Trail

The longest, and arguably most scenic, rail-trail in California, this spectacular path runs between Westwood and Susanville in Lassen County. It cuts through the thick woodlands of the high country into the majestic Susan River Canyon, passing numerous historic sites such as tunnels and trestles along the way.

The Bizz Johnson National Recreation Trail follows the route of the old Fernley and Lassen Railroad line, which was established in 1914 for transporting logs and milled lumber to and from the Westwood Mill. The mill closed in 1956, and in 1978, Southern Pacific Railroad received approval to discontinue use of the old rail line. The federal Bureau of Land Management spearheaded conversion of the corridor to a trail, and former California congressional representative Harold T. "Bizz" Johnson, who served in the House of Representatives from 1958 to 1980, was instrumental in establishing the

The Bizz Johnson National Recreation Trail follows the bends of the Susan River for 16 miles of trail's length.

Location
Lassen County

Endpoints
Susanville to Westwood

Mileage
25.4

Roughness Index
3

Surface
Gravel, ballast

33

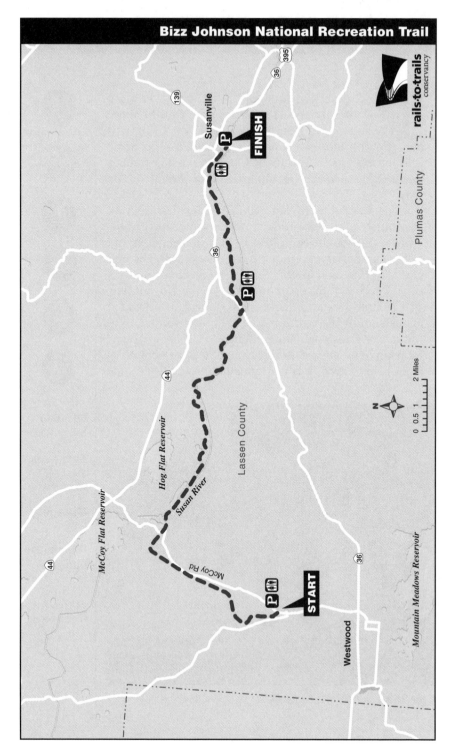

Named to Rails-to-Trails Conservancy's Rail-Trail Hall of Fame, the rural Bizz Johnson is known for it trail tunnels.

segment as a rails-to-trails conversion for recreational use. The trail is named in his honor.

Heading from Westwood to Susanville, the route is mainly flat or slightly downhill. You are surrounded by open forest for the first 4.5 miles, and then you follow the Susan River for the last 16 miles. As it winds through the rugged Susan River Canyon, the trail crosses the river 12 times on bridges and trestles and passes through two tunnels. The landscape is a combination of semiarid canyon and upland forests of pine and fir. Beyond the canyon, the trail follows existing roads an additional 4.5 miles into Westwood, where a railroad station-type kiosk and a 25-foot carved redwood statue of Paul Bunyan mark the Westwood trailhead.

In the spring and early summer, trail users can hike, mountain bike and horseback ride on the Bizz Johnson. Another highlight is camping along and fishing in the Susan River for rainbow and brown trout in the spring and early summer. Visitors can camp along the trail on Bureau of Land Management and U.S. Forest Service lands for up to seven days unless otherwise posted. The camping is primitive, and permits are required for campfires. In the winter months, 18.5 miles of the trail are open for cross-country skiing. If possible, plan your visit to coincide with the annual three-day Rails to Trails Festival, which takes place at the Susanville Depot in early October and includes live music, a barbecue, railroad handcar rides and other activities that are great for families.

DIRECTIONS

Take Highway 36 to Westwood, turn north onto Lassen County Road A-21/Mooney Road and continue 3 miles to County Road 101/McCoy Road (just before the railroad tracks). Follow County Rd. 101 a half mile until you reach Mason Station trailhead. There is ample parking at the station. You will see a large sign with trail brochures near a restroom and the trailhead. Follow the path from the trailhead for a quarter mile until you reach the railroad grade.

To reach the Susanville Depot, follow Highway 36, which becomes Main Street in Susanville. Continue on Main Street through Historic Uptown Susanville to Weatherlow Street, at the first stoplight at the base of the hill. Turn right on Weatherlow (which becomes Richmond Road) and continue a half mile to the Susanville Railroad Depot Trailhead Visitor Center. The trail begins at the depot, which has parking.

Contact: The Bureau of Land Management
Eagle Lake
2950 Riverside Drive
Susanville, CA 96130
(530) 257-0456
www.blm.gov/ca/st/en/fo/eaglelake/bizztrail.html

Black Diamond Railroad Trail

Black Diamond Mines Regional Preserve is a splendid place with a fascinating and unique history. From the 1850s to the early 1900s, the region was the site of the largest coal mining operation in California. People from all over the world migrated here, and the coalfield's presence transformed the area from one primarily used for cattle ranching into the industrial and population center of Contra Costa County. Mining operations ceased in the late 1940s due to dwindling profits, and the land reverted to agricultural use once again.

In the late 1970s the East Bay Regional Park District started to acquire the property to create Black Diamond Mines Regional Preserve. Today, the preserve totals almost 6,000 acres, supports a diverse wildlife population, offers visitors a variety of activities and is a primary destination for Bay Area nature-lovers. Some of the fascinating sites that can be explored here include original mine openings, a cemetery and a visitor center that contains

The Black Diamond Railroad Trail, though short, provides a glimpse of the preserve's cattle ranching and later coal mining history.

Location
Contra Costa County

Endpoints
Large parking lot to small parking lot, both on Somersville Road

Mileage
0.8

Roughness Index
3

Surface
Dirt

37

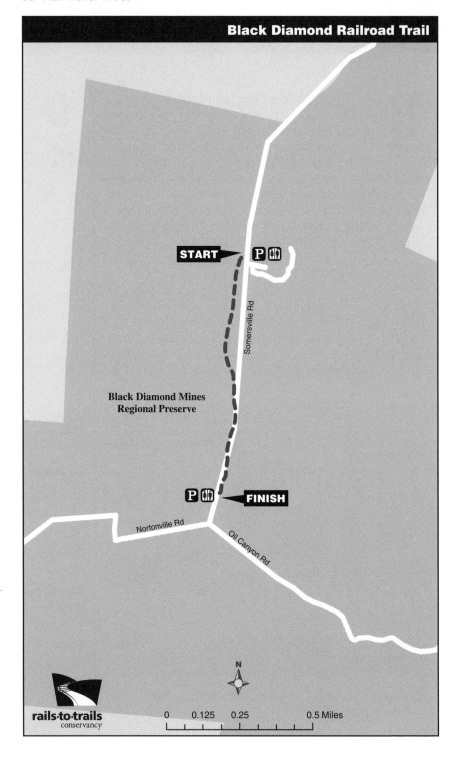

displays, photographs, videos, brochures and artifacts depicting the park's mining eras.

The preserve contains some 65 miles of trails. One of these, the Black Diamond Railroad Trail, is a short rail-trail that can be explored by bicycle or on foot. Its length and very slight incline makes it ideal for people of all ages. There is no shade along the trail, though, so be sure to bring plenty of water and protection from the sun.

The trailhead is located at the south end of the main parking lot, where there are restrooms, water fountains and literature about the preserve and its history. Once you step onto the rail-trail, you are surrounded by the expansive Mt. Diablo foothills. On the left is a steep canyon, which is covered with lush green glass and bright yellow wildflowers in spring. On the right is a ravine and Somersville Road, which parallels the rail-trail its entire length. Look beyond the road for a vista of rolling hills, where cattle, rabbits and deer roam. The canyon grows slightly narrower you ascend it. At the trail's end there is a rest area with picnic tables, restrooms and a small parking lot. It is the perfect place to sit down, have a snack and enjoy the peaceful surroundings. You can turn around or continue hiking; unpaved trails of various lengths branch out from this point.

DIRECTIONS

To reach the northern trailhead, take Highway 4 to the Somersville Road exit in Antioch, then drive south (toward the hills) on Somersville Rd. until it enters Black Diamond Mines Regional Preserve. Continue another mile or so to the park entrance station and park in the lot. The trailhead is located at the south end of the main parking lot.

To reach the southern trailhead, continue on Somersville Rd. past the visitor center for another mile and you will come to a small parking lot. You can park here to access the rail-trail from the south end.

Contact: East Bay Regional Parks
5175 Somersville Road
Antioch, CA 94509
(925) 757-2620
www.ebparks.org/parks/black_diamond

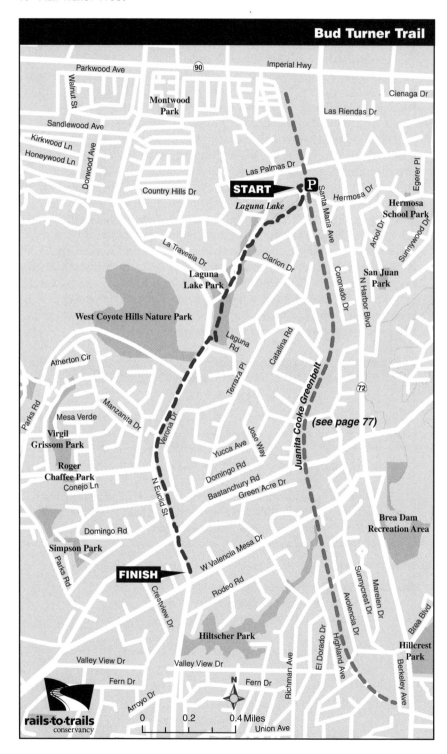

Bud Turner Trail

Parkwood Ave

90

Imperial Hwy

Cienaga Dr

Walnut St

Montwood Park

Las Riendas Dr

Sandlewood Ave

Kirkwood Ln

Honeywood Ln

Dorwood Ave

Egerer Pl

Country Hills Dr

Las Palmas Dr

START P

Hermosa Dr

Hermosa School Park

Laguna Lake

Santa Maria Ave

Arbol Dr

Sunnywood Dr

La Travesia Dr

Clarion Dr

Laguna Lake Park

Coronado Dr

N Harbor Blvd

San Juan Park

West Coyote Hills Nature Park

Laguna Rd

Catalina Rd

Atherton Cir

Terraza Pl

72

Parks Rd

Mesa Verde

Manzanita Dr

Verona Dr

Jose Way

Juanita Cooke Greenbelt

(see page 77)

Virgil Grissom Park

Yucca Ave

N Euclid St

Roger Chaffee Park

Conejo Ln

Domingo Rd

Bastanchury Rd

Green Acre Dr

Brea Dam Recreation Area

Domingo Rd

Simpson Park

Parks Rd

FINISH

W Valencia Mesa Dr

Rodeo Rd

Sunnycrest Dr

Avolencia Dr

Marelen Dr

Brea Blvd

Crestview Dr

Hiltscher Park

El Dorado Dr

Highland Ave

Hillcrest Park

Valley View Dr

Valley View Dr

Richman Ave

Berkeley Ave

Fern Dr

N

Fern Dr

Arroyo Dr

0   0.2   0.4 Miles

Union Ave

rails·to·trails
conservancy

Bud Turner Trail

Experience the easy life of the West Coast on Orange County's Bud Turner Trail. Set in a quiet neighborhood in the city of Fullerton, the trail is ideal for all types of trail use and uniquely caters to equestrian use. The trail connects to the Juanita Cooke Greenbelt (page 77), which provides access to other parts of the city.

Through his leadership role with the Fullerton Recreational Riders, a local equestrian organization, Bud Turner was influential in getting this trail built and that is why this great trail is named after him. The Juanita Cooke Greenbelt also bears the name of a former leader of the Fullerton Recreational Riders.

Linked to the Juanita Cooke Greenbelt, the Bud Turner Trail is a peaceful community pathway where you're as likely to see neighbors on horseback as on bicycles.

Beginning at the north end of Laguna Lake Park, the trail skirts the southern edge of the lake to head southwest. This peaceful, grassy lakefront park is a great place to have a picnic or try out your fishing pole. It's also where the Bud Turner Trail and the Juanita Cooke Greenbelt connect. Just beyond the lake you come to an equestrian riding ring—don't be surprised to catch a glimpse of locals on horseback as this is a popular equestrian area. After passing the ring you go through a pleasant neighborhood before connecting with North Euclid Street. The trail runs alongside this busy road the rest of the way. Take caution, as you will need to cross some major intersections, including one at West Bastanchury Road.

The trail ends near downtown Fullerton, close to the intersection of North Euclid Street and West Valencia Mesa Drive. From here you can connect to the historic

Location
Orange County

Endpoints
Laguna Lake Park to Euclid Street and West Valencia Mesa Drive

Mileage
1.8

Roughness Index
2

Surface
Woodchips, dirt

downtown district to the south, which has restaurants and shops in a laid-back Southern California setting.

DIRECTIONS

To reach the Laguna Lake Park trailhead, take the Euclid Street exit from California 91 (the Riverside Freeway) in Fullerton. Head (right or left) north on Euclid Street for about 4 miles to Lakeview Road. Turn right (east) on Lakeview Road and go 0.5 mile to Hermosa Drive. Turn right (east) on Hermosa Drive and go 0.1 mile to Lakeside Drive. The entrance to Laguna Lake Park is at this intersection, and there is parking along the street.

The other endpoint of this trail is a street intersection and, therefore, not a formal trailhead.

Contact: Orange County Transportation Authority
550 South Main Street
P.O. Box 14184
Orange, CA 92868
(714) 636-RIDE (7433)
www.octa.net

Chandler Bikeway

The Chandler Bikeway is a jewel tucked nicely into a Burbank neighborhood. The bikeway begins as a well-maintained corridor that runs in the median between the lanes of traffic on Chandler Boulevard. The trail sits on top of the old Burbank Branch of the Southern Pacific Transportation Company Railroad. While this section of the trail is uniquely situated between traffic lanes, it is surprisingly beautiful, with extensive landscaping, including a wide array of trees, shrubs and flower beds dotting the grounds surrounding the trail. A varied group of users make use of the bikeway, and the trail is well-marked with separate bicycle and pedestrian lanes painted on the pavement.

The first 2 miles are defined by the quaint and tidy neighborhood that it passes through. The area is made up of unique homes, some with very bright and vibrant paint jobs that remind you that you are in sunny Southern California. The abundance of orange and lemon trees

The Chandler Bikeway is heralded as a trail gem and a 2.8-mile testament to thoughtful urban use and community development.

Location
Los Angeles County

Endpoints
Chandler Boulevard and North Mariposa Street to Chandler Boulevard and Vineland Avenue

Mileage
2.8

Roughness Index
1

Surface
Asphalt

43

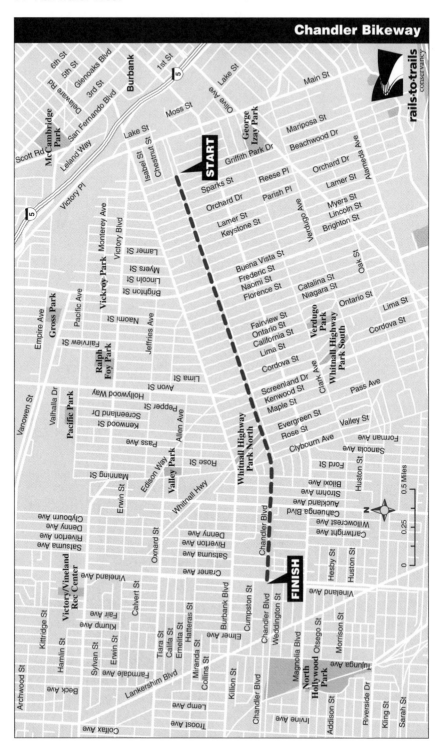

in residents yards also make for a wonderful sight in the winter. Another treat along this section are the two sculptures that appear along the trail.

Upon crossing Clybourn Avenue via crosswalk, you have left the city limits of Burbank and entered North Hollywood. The trail now shifts to the side of the road and out of the middle median. The surrounding cityscape changes as well from residential neighborhoods to light industrial and retail development. The public art on display along this final mile of trail is second to none along any rail-trail. A collection of murals adorn the sides of the buildings between Clybourn Avenue and the trails end at Vineland Avenue. The murals were commissioned by L.A. Mayor Richard Riordan's Targeted Neighborhood Initiative Program and were created by 19 local artists. The artworks honor subjects from the movie industry to music, nature, railroads and the bountiful harvest from the lush farms of California. The trail ends at Vineland Avenue after about 2.8 miles of wonderful riding and is an excellent example of land use and community development at its finest.

DIRECTIONS

To reach the eastern trailhead from Interstate 5, take the West Burbank Boulevard exit and take a left onto West Burbank Blvd. After just 0.3 mile take a left onto Victory Boulevard. After another quarter mile take a right onto West Chandler Boulevard. The trailhead with on-street parking is another quarter mile up Chandler Blvd.

To reach the western trailhead from I-5, take the West Burbank Boulevard exit and take a left onto West Burbank Blvd. After 3.2 miles, take a left onto Vineland Avenue. The trailhead (with on-street parking) is a quarter mile away on the left at the intersection with Chandler Boulevard.

Contact: Friends of the Chandler Bikeway
Park, Recreation and Community Services Department
301 East Olive Avenue
Burbank, CA 91502
(818) 238-5378
http://chandlerbikewayburbank.com

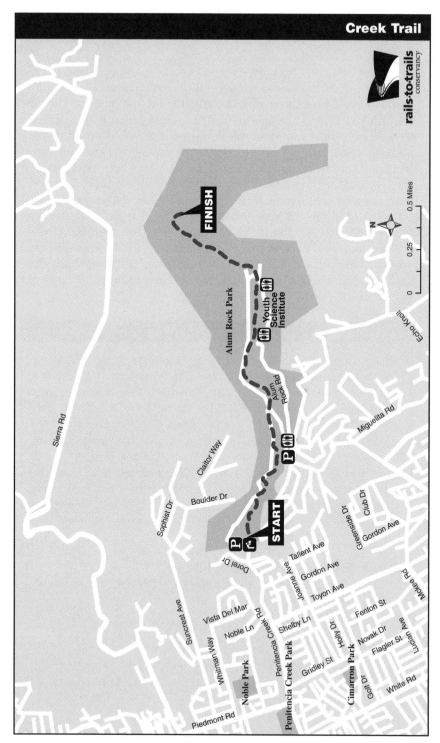

Creek Trail

rails-to-trails
conservancy

FINISH

Alum Rock Park

Youth Science Institute

Alum Rock Rd

Sierra Rd

Claitor Way

Boulder Dr

Sophist Dr

P

P

START

Dorel Dr

Miguelita Rd

Echo Knoll

Greenside Dr

Club Dr

Gordon Ave

Tallent Ave

Joanne Ave

Gordon Ave

Toyon Ave

McKee Rd

Suncrest Ave

Vista Del Mar

Whitman Way

Noble Ln

Penitencia Creek Rd

Shelby Ln

Gridley St

Holly Dr

Fenton St

Novak Dr

Flagler St Ave

Lucian Ave

White Rd

Golf Dr

Cimarron Park

Penitencia Creek Park

Noble Park

Piedmont Rd

N

0   0.25   0.5 Miles

Creek Trail

Nestled between Alum Rock Canyon and the Mt. Diablo foothills, Alum Rock Park near Santa Clara is California's oldest city park. From the early to mid-1900s it was a popular resort and spa, complete with an indoor swimming pool, mineral baths and a restaurant. Visitors rode a train from San Jose into the park until the late 1920s, when the railroad folded.

Alum Rock Park's 2.4-mile Creek Trail follows a portion of the old tourist railroad line. It is a great family rail-trail, offering an abundance of modern facilities while maintaining its natural beauty and unique geological formations. The paved portion of the trail is wheelchair accessible.

Stone bridges and nearby grottos along the Creek Trail are reminders of the area's former appeal as a spa and resort destination.

The trail begins as a dirt track with a fairly steep incline as it heads out into the park but quickly levels out. On the left are rolling hills and the Penitencia Creek, its banks blanketed with several types of fern as well as blackberry and wild rosebushes. On the right is a steep, fern-covered canyon.

The scenery begins to change after about a half mile, as signs of civilization emerge. You pass the shaded Quail Hollow picnic area and a campground. The surface becomes paved and smooth 1.4 miles in. Continuing on to mile 1.5, you see a visitor center that features a ranger station, picnic benches, open spaces for sports and horseshoe pits. There are two playgrounds nearby, one on each side of the visitor center. One has tot swings and is designed for smaller children. The other has larger equipment for older kids.

Location
Santa Clara County

Endpoints
Penitencia Creek Road in Alum Rock Park to Alum Rock Park

Mileage
2.4

Roughness Index
3

Surface
Dirt

The Youth Science Institute (YSI) is located 2 miles in. It runs summer camps for children and houses a variety of live animals for display throughout the year. Farther along on the left are several beautiful old stone bridges and small grottos. The grottos were constructed in the early 1900s to enclose the park's mineral springs. These springs were believed to possess healing properties, and their presence played a major role in the early success of Alum Rock Park. Signs posted in front of the grottos give detailed information about the springs and their history.

The rail-trail begins to feel rustic again toward the end. The surface changes to dirt, and the trail becomes enveloped by a variety of trees, including coast live oak, madrone and sycamore. Soon you arrive at a wood-plank steel bridge that crosses the creek. This is the end of the rail-trail, and bicycles are not allowed beyond this point. If you are on foot, you can cross this bridge and continue walking, where you'll eventually meet up with the South Rim Trail. A complete trail map is available on Alum Rock Park's website: www.sjparks. org/Parks/RegionalParks/arp/index.asp.

DIRECTIONS

From Interstate 680 take Berryessa Road east. Turn right onto Piedmont Road, then left on Penitencia Creek Road. Continue past a residential area on Penitencia Creek Road until you come to a dead end with a parking lot and signed trailhead.

Contact: Alum Rock Park
200 East Santa Clara Street
San Jose, CA 95113
(408) 535-3570
www.sjparks.org/Parks/RegionalParks/arp/index.asp

Delta Meadows River Park

While the trail in Delta Meadows River Park is relatively short, it remains one of the more interesting rail-trail destinations in California. It appeals to a variety of enthusiasts, including photographers, birders, anglers, hikers, historians and naturalists. Located in the northern Sacramento-San Joaquin River Delta near the historic delta towns of Locke and Walnut Grove, the park's maze of channels, sloughs and islands offers a refreshing glimpse of what the region looked like hundreds of years ago.

Make sure to bring your camera and binoculars (and possibly a fishing rod) because the area is teeming with wildlife, including beavers, river otters, muskrats, black-tailed deer, blue herons, kingfishers and mallards. The trail runs very close to the waters of the delta, so you'll be in a great position for spotting animals. If you'd like to learn more about the area, you can take a guided canoe ride along the river. The Delta Natural History

The Delta Meadows River Park is ideal for wildlife watchers wanting to catch glimpses of river otters, kingfishers, muskrats and mallards.

Location
Sacramento County

Endpoints
Delta Meadows River Park

Mileage
1

Roughness Index
2

Surface
Ballast, dirt

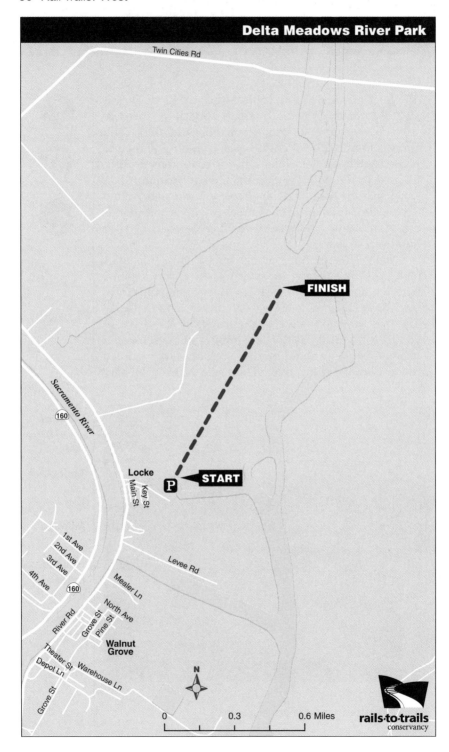

Association provides guides in the spring and fall: Reservations can be made through Brannan Island State Park (916-777-6671).

The trail is certainly bikeable, but you're probably better off walking. The trail is short, and you'll want to take your time to see what you can discover along the trail without the hassle of bringing your bike. There are plenty of other pathways within the park to explore as well.

On your way out of town, you might want to stop in nearby Walnut Grove or Locke for a taste of delta history. Walnut Grove, which today hosts a number of small shops, was one of the first settlements along the Sacramento River. It was also home to a vibrant Chinese community. A 1916 fire destroyed Walnut Grove's Chinatown, leading to the development of nearby Locke. Locke remains one of only a handful of towns in the U.S. that was built entirely by Chinese hands. Today, the California State Park System is in the process of converting an old Chinese boarding house in Locke into a museum that will document the important role the Chinese played in developing the delta levee system.

DIRECTIONS

From Interstate 5, take exit 498 for Twin Cities Road toward Walnut Grove/Galt, turning right onto Twin Cities Road. Travel 4 miles and turn left onto River Road. Travel about 2 miles, then turn left onto Levee Road, just before the bridge. (If you reach the town of Walnut Grove, you've gone too far.) After turning onto Levee Road, make the first left and look for signs to Delta Meadows River Park. Travel on the park access road for about 0.5 mile until you reach a gate. The unmarked trail starts on the other side of the gate.

Contact: California State Parks
Gold Fields District
17645 State Highway 160
Rio Vista, CA 94571
(916) 777-7701

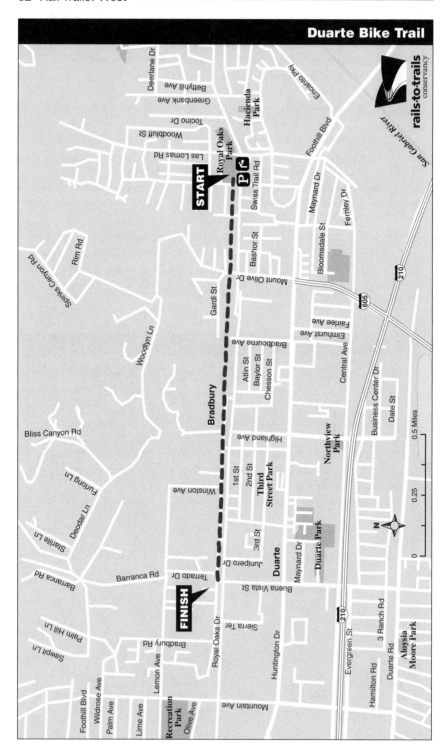

Duarte Bike Trail

rails·to·trails
conservancy

San Gabriel River

START

FINISH

Royal Oaks Park

Hacienda Park

Street Park

Northview Park

Duarte Park

Recreation Park

Aloysia Moore Park

Bradbury

Third

Duarte

N

0   0.25   0.5 Miles

Duarte Bike Trail

T he Duarte Bike (or Multipurpose) Trail is made up of paved and parallel dirt trails. Connecting a park, a school and a hospital, it is a wonderful example of a recreation path, transportation corridor and safe route to school. The trail hosts a wide array of users, including walkers, bikers, inline skaters and even some horseback riders on the dirt path.

You'll want to start out at the eastern trailhead, at Royal Oaks Park, because there is ample parking here. The park offers many facilities for young and old, including basketball and tennis courts, short walking paths and playground equipment. On the right are dramatic views of the San Gabriel Mountains and Angeles National Forest. As it leaves Royal Oaks Park, the trail is a well-maintained concrete pathway. Soon you pass a school that sits back to the right, where children at play provide pleasant background noise.

A parallel dirt path for equestrians and asphalt trail surface make the Duarte Bike Trail a friendly path for multiuse recreation.

Location
Los Angeles County

Endpoints
Royal Oaks Park to Buena Vista Street

Mileage
1.6

Roughness Index
1

Surface
Asphalt

Not far beyond the school is one of the jewels of the trail, a large bridge that provides access over the trail to a connecting neighborhood. In season a profusion of wildflowers spreads across this picturesque spot. If you take the few minutes to walk to the top of the bridge, you will be rewarded with an exceptional view of wildflowers and the trail. A few benches and water fountains line the trail.

Located in Southern California's San Gabriel Valley, Duarte is named for Andres Duarte, a Mexican soldier who was granted the land in the 1840s while it was still in Mexican ownership.

DIRECTIONS

To reach the eastern trailhead, from Interstate 605 (the San Gabriel River Freeway) travel north to just past Interstate 210, where I-605 becomes Mt. Olive Drive. Follow Mt. Olive Drive 1,350 feet and turn right on Royal Oaks Drive. Follow Royal Oaks Drive for 0.5 mile; Royal Oaks Park, which has parking, will be on the left.

To reach the western trailhead, from I-605 travel north to just past I-210, where I-605 becomes Mt. Olive Drive. Follow Mt. Olive Drive 1,350 feet and turn left on Royal Oaks Drive. Follow Royal Oaks Drive for 1.25 miles. The trailhead is on the right at the corner of Royal Oaks Drive and Buena Vista Street. On-street parking is available nearby.

Contact: Duarte City Hall
1600 Huntington Drive
Duarte, CA 91010
(626) 357-7931
www.accessduarte.com/ParksandRecreation/
index.asp

Fairfield Linear Park

Running from Solano Community College, on the southwest edge of town, into the town of Fairfield, this path provides convenient bike access to the action on campus and in the city center.

Once it leaves the college, the first 3 miles of the path follow closely beside Interstate 80 through open farmland, passing some light industrial areas along the way. In this section, the path is fenced on both sides, so there is limited access. Mature trees provide considerable shade, and bicycle bridges provide passage across several small streams.

At about the 3-mile mark the trail crosses under Interstate 80 and abruptly changes character. The surface changes from asphalt to concrete, streetlights appear, and the trail winds through quiet residential subdivisions. There is easy trail access at multiple points on this section, as well as plenty of benches and picnic tables, and two tot playgrounds. The area is extensively landscaped and well-maintained, providing a pleasant parklike atmosphere. Nearby residents make full use of this part of the trail for dog walking, biking, evening strolls and family gatherings. The trail ends near the Solano Mall, in an open grassy park complete with a rose garden.

You can't ask for a more pleasant commuter route than the Fairfield Linear Park's flower- and tree-lined path.

If you're in Fairfield in mid-August, check out their popular Tomato Festival and West Coast Barbeque Championship. You're also very close to several wineries in Suisun Valley.

Location
Solano County

Endpoints
Solano Mall
Road and Travis
Boulevard to
Suisun Valley Road

Mileage
4.4

**Roughness
Index**
1

Surface
Asphalt

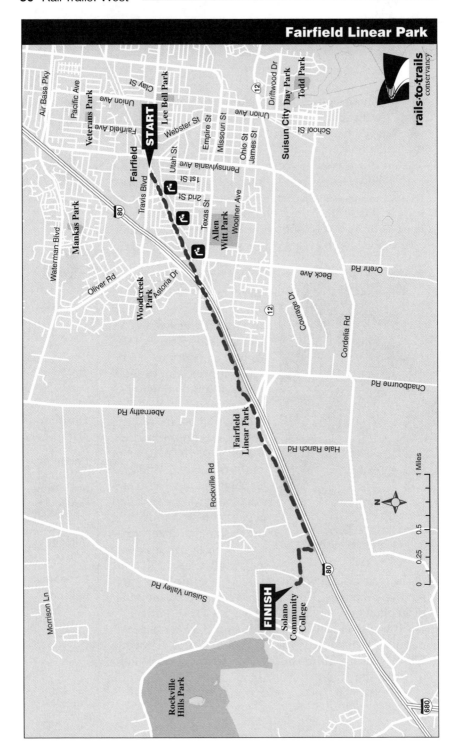

DIRECTIONS

To reach the Solano Community College trailhead, exit Interstate 80 at Abernathy Road, and go north for 0.5 mile. You will cross over the bike path, which is adjacent to I-80. At 1.7 miles turn left on Rockville Road. Proceed to Suisun Valley Road, and turn left. Go 0.3 mile to Solano Community College. The bike path starts at the rear of the large campus, behind the soccer fields and adjacent to a small bridge leading over a culvert to the school baseball field.

To reach the Solano Mall trailhead, exit I-80 at Travis Boulevard. Go east 0.5 mile to Solano Mall. There is ample parking at Solano Mall. The trail starts at the PARCOURSE sign in the grassy park area on the other side of Travis Boulevard, near the intersection of Solano Mall Road and Travis Boulevard. Solano Mall Road is one of the main entrances to the mall; a traffic light aids in crossing busy Travis Boulevard.

Contact: City of Fairfield
Community Service Department
1000 Webster Street
Fairfield, CA 94533
(707) 428-7465

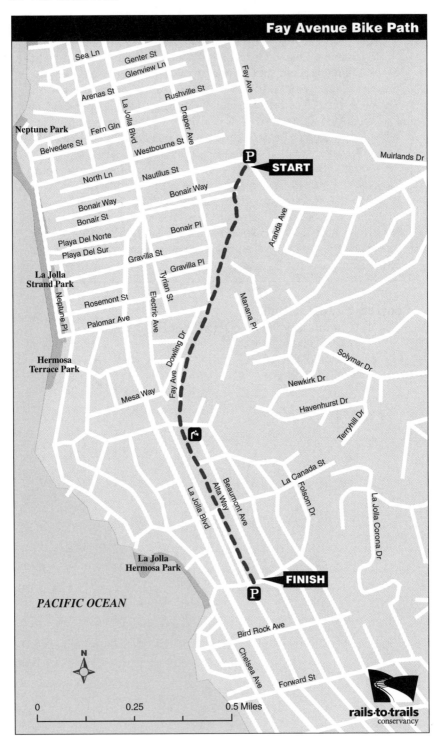

Fay Avenue Bike Path

Make sure you bring your camera for this trail. The Fay Avenue Bike Path runs through the upscale seaside resort community of La Jolla, and opens up to the sweeping vistas of the Pacific Ocean, abundant palm trees and terra cotta rooftops that give Southern California its intoxicating charm.

Starting out by La Jolla High School, the trail winds through a pleasantly landscaped neighborhood. From the trail you can take in the ocean air and enjoy striking views of the coast below. A quiet neighborhood park offers a playground, water fountain and several grassy, shaded areas for relaxing. Beyond the park, prickly pear cacti and agave plants dot the landscape, and mature eucalyptus trees nicely frame the path. The trail weaves its way past a number of houses whose owners have made their own contributions to the trail's aesthetic appeal, with a variety of plantings, shrubs and ornate fences.

So Cal charm is in abundance on the Fay Avenue Bike Path, a rail-trail with Pacific Ocean vistas and terracotta-roofed neighborhoods.

Location
San Diego County

Endpoints
Fay Avenue and Nautilus Street to Camino de la Costa and La Jolla Hermosa Avenue

Mileage
1.1

Roughness Index
1

Surface
Asphalt, dirt

The trail, which runs along the former San Diego, Pacific Beach and La Jolla Railroad line, is mainly paved with asphalt, but toward the end it turns into a dirt path. If you're careful, you can still negotiate the entire route on a road bike if the surface is dry. The trail officially ends at La Jolla Hermosa Avenue but continues as an on-street bike path that connects to other bike facilities.

While the Fay Avenue Bike Path is short, it provides a rich experience of breathtaking views, ocean air and eye-pleasing landscaping, making it well worth a visit.

DIRECTIONS

From downtown San Diego, follow Interstate 5 North, take exit 26A and merge onto Ardath Road/La Jolla Parkway. Follow Ardath Road for 1.2 miles, and then make a slight left onto Torrey Pines Road. After 1.5 miles, turn left onto Girard Avenue. Make a right onto Genter Street and a quick left onto Fay Avenue. Park on Fay Avenue outside the La Jolla High School Aquatic Center, near Nautilus Street. The trailhead is located on the opposite side of Nautilus Street, just west of the intersection of Fay Avenue and Nautilus Street.

Contact: City of San Diego
1010 Second Avenue, Suite 800
San Diego, CA 92101
(619) 533-3126

Fresno-Clovis Rail-Trail

Community support has been integral to the creation of the Fresno Sugar Pine Trail and the Clovis Old Town Trail. Joggers, cyclists, businesses, and multiple environmental organizations all came together to support this rail-trail, which runs 13 miles through Clovis and Fresno. It connects many existing area resources, including the Yosemite International Airport, Woodward Park and the 23-mile San Joaquin River Parkway Trail. Through tree planting efforts organized by the Coalition for Community Trails, about 4,400 trees planted along it offer trail users shade and beautiful scenery.

Known collectively as the Fresno-Clovis Rail-Trail, this path was created by combining two separate railroad corridors and stretches from southern Clovis to northern edge of Fresno. The portion in Fresno is known as the Sugar Pine Trail, and once it enters Clovis it is referred to as the Clovis Old Town Trail. The Clovis Old

A trail made of many parts and many names, the Fresno-Clovis Rail-Trail network has been embraced as an important community connector.

Location
Fresno County

Endpoints
Clovis to Fresno

Mileage
13

Roughness Index
1

Surface
Asphalt

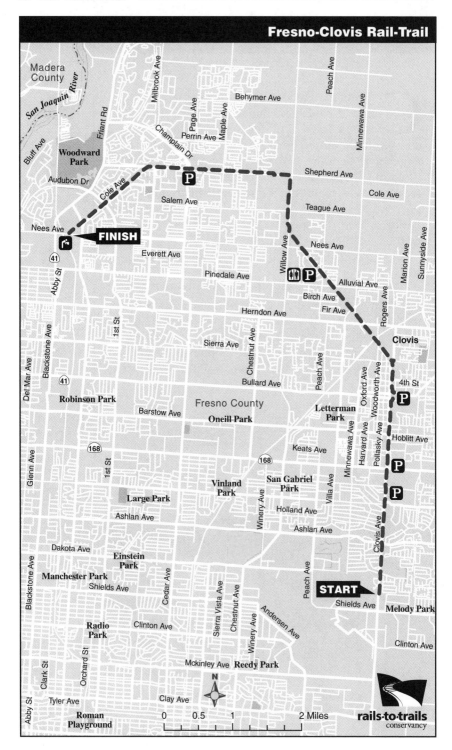

Fresno-Clovis Rail-Trail

Madera County

San Joaquin River

Woodward Park

Millbrook Ave

Page Ave

Maple Ave

Behymer Ave

Peach Ave

Minnewawa Ave

Friant Rd

Champlain Dr

Perrin Ave

Bluff Ave

Audubon Dr

Cole Ave

Shepherd Ave

Cole Ave

Salem Ave

Teague Ave

Nees Ave

FINISH

41

Abby St

Everett Ave

Pinedale Ave

Willow Ave

Nees Ave

Marion Ave

Sunnyside Ave

Alluvial Ave

Birch Ave

Fir Ave

Rogers Ave

Herndon Ave

Blackstone Ave

1st St

Sierra Ave

Chestnut Ave

Clovis

Del Mar Ave

41

Bullard Ave

Peach Ave

Oxford Ave

Woodworth Ave

4th St

Robinson Park

Barstow Ave

Fresno County

Oneill Park

Letterman Park

Harvard Ave

Pollasky Ave

Hoblitt Ave

168

1st St

Keats Ave

Minnewawa Ave

Glenn Ave

168

Vinland Park

San Gabriel Park

Villa Ave

Large Park

Winery Ave

Holland Ave

Ashlan Ave

Clovis Ave

Ashlan Ave

Dakota Ave

Einstein Park

Manchester Park

Shields Ave

Cedar Ave

Sierra Vista Ave

Chestnut Ave

Peach Ave

START

Melody Park

Radio Park

Clinton Ave

Winery Ave

Andersen Ave

Shields Ave

Clinton Ave

Blackstone Ave

Clark St

Orchard St

Mckinley Ave

Reedy Park

N

Abby St

Tyler Ave

Roman Playground

Clay Ave

0   0.5   1   2 Miles

rails·to·trails
conservancy

Town Trail begins near the Yosemite International Airport and continues north along Clovis Avenue. The Clovis Old Town Trail officially becomes the Fresno Sugar Pine Trail on Willow Avenue between Nees Avenue and East Shepherd Avenue, which leads westward along East Shepherd Avenue to the River Park Shopping Center in Fresno. In Fresno, the trail begins at Fresno Street and Nees Avenue and runs along Eriant Road to Shepherd, then east to Willow Avenue. The trail runs south along Willow Avenue and continues southeast into Clovis. Underpasses carry the trail through busy intersections in Clovis and Fresno.

The Clovis Old Town Trail skirts many residential and commercial areas, with easy access along the entire length. Outdoor restaurants at Willow Station, a new commercial mall area at Willow and Nees in Clovis, offer seating overlooking the trail, and additional restaurants and stores are within walking distance to the trail as it continues near Shepherd Road. The trail transitions from commercial to residential near the end, becoming a wide and spacious corridor bordered by mature trees. It ends at River Park Shopping Center in Fresno, a large mall complex near the intersection of Highway 41 and Nees Avenue. The trailhead is under the Highway 41 overpass, and is equipped with benches and a drinking fountain. There is ample parking and a wide choice of eateries at the mall across the street.

DIRECTIONS

To reach the southern trailhead in Clovis, from Highway 99, exit at CA-180E, proceed 7 miles to exit at 63 (Clovis Avenue) and then head north for 2.5 miles. The trailhead is on Clovis Avenue, 0.3 mile south of the intersection with Dakota Avenue. There is no parking at the trailhead, but users can park along Dakota Avenue.

To reach the northern trailhead in Fresno, from Highway 41, exit at CA-135 (Friant Road/Blackstone Avenue). Go south on Friant/Blackstone 0.5 mile, and turn left on West Nees Avenue. The trailhead will be on your left, under the freeway overpass. There is no parking at the trailhead, but you will find ample parking at River Park Mall, on your right.

Contact: City of Clovis
Public Utilities Department
155 North Sunnyside Avenue
Clovis, CA 93611
(559) 324-2620
www.ci.clovis.ca.us

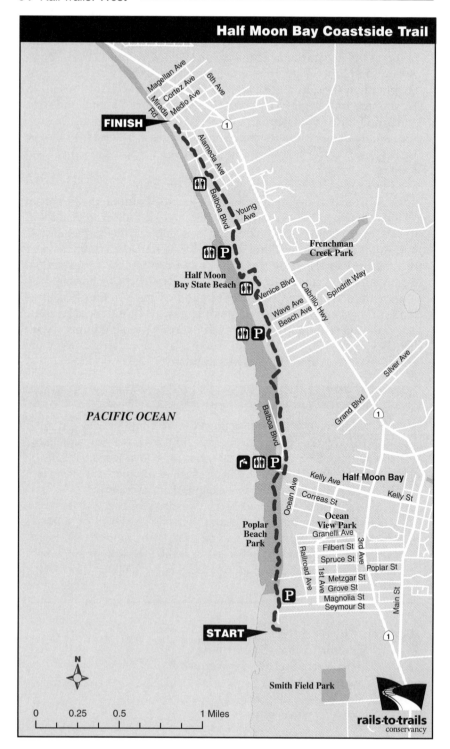

Half Moon Bay Coastside Trail

FINISH

Magellan Ave
Cortez Ave
Mirada Rd
Medio Ave
6th Ave
Alameda Ave
Balboa Blvd
Young Ave

Frenchman
Creek Park

Half Moon
Bay State Beach

Venice Blvd
Wave Ave
Beach Ave
Cabrillo Hwy
Spindrift Way

PACIFIC OCEAN

Balboa Blvd

Silver Ave

Grand Blvd

Half Moon Bay

Kelly Ave
Kelly St

Ocean Ave
Correas St

Ocean
View Park
Granelli Ave

Poplar
Beach
Park

Railroad Ave
Filbert St
Spruce St
Metzgar St
Grove St
Magnolia St
Seymour St
1st Ave
3rd Ave
Poplar St
Main St

START

N

Smith Field Park

0   0.25   0.5   1 Miles

rails·to·trails
conservancy

Half Moon Bay Coastside Trail

Half Moon Bay State Park's Coastside Trail runs parallel to the Pacific Coast along what used to be the Ocean Shore Railroad. The railroad itself was in operation for just 14 years before it was driven out of business in the early 1920s by the automobile. However, the railroad had a tremendous impact on the Northern California coastline. It opened the area to agriculture, created new communities along the shoreline, and made the coastal beaches prime tourist destinations.

The Coastside Trail is truly a destination trail. It offers users sweeping views of the Pacific Ocean, access to several beaches and excellent nature viewing. Bird watching is quite good and a popular activity here. Red-tailed hawks, blue herons and red-winged blackbirds are spotted frequently, and large hawks can often be seen perched on benches and the trail's split-rail fence. Half Moon Bay State Beach is also home of the world-famous Mavericks, a surfing spot near Pillar Point that's visible

Location
San Mateo
County

Endpoints
Seymour Bridge
to Mirada Road

Mileage
3.5

**Roughness
Index**
1

Surface
Asphalt

The Half Moon Bay Coastside Trail follows the spectacularly scenic route of the Ocean Shore Railroad and serves as a beach playground as much as a pathway.

from the trail. In winter, surfers can ride waves up to 80 feet high here.

You can park at the Half Moon Bay State Beach Visitor Center for a $6 day-use fee and pick up the trail here. Heading north you follow the paved trail for about 2 miles in total. On your left is the coastline, and on your right, the equestrian trail. Beyond this trail are views of gorgeous beachfront properties. A mile into your walk, you reach another parking lot with access to Venice Beach. The rail-trail continues for about another mile from this point, then merges into Mirada Road. If you continue walking on Mirada Road for a few minutes, you will end up at the Miramar Beach Restaurant, a bar and restaurant that overlooks the ocean. This is a great place to watch the sunset—the Miramar even posts a daily sunset schedule on its website.

Heading south from the visitor center, the Pacific Ocean is on your right and the equestrian trail on your left. Beyond this horse trail are open, green fields. The trail hugs the bluff's edge here. As you head south you see a landscape of wind-sculpted trees. It is typically windy along the bluff, so be sure to bring a jacket for this leg of the trail. The rail-trail officially ends about 1 mile in, and the surface changes to dirt. However, you can continue walking south along the cliff's edge, as there is still a path to follow. This path, which the Coastside Trail is also a part of, is a segment of the much longer California Coastal Trail. The Coastal Trail is currently about halfway completed and will eventually run along the entire coast of California.

DIRECTIONS

To reach the Half Moon Bay State Beach Visitor Center, take CA Highway 1 and turn onto Kelly Avenue toward the coast. The visitor center is at the end of Kelly Avenue. Park in the visitor center parking lot. There is no parking at the endpoints.

Additional parking is available at Venice Beach, at the end of Venice Boulevard off Highway 1, and Dunes Beach, at the end of Young Avenue off Highway 1.

Contact: Half Moon Bay State Beach
95 Kelly Avenue
Half Moon Bay, CA 94019
(650) 726-8819
www.parks.ca.gov/default.asp?page_id=531

Hammond Coastal Trail

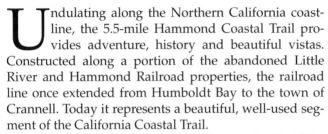

Undulating along the Northern California coastline, the 5.5-mile Hammond Coastal Trail provides adventure, history and beautiful vistas. Constructed along a portion of the abandoned Little River and Hammond Railroad properties, the railroad line once extended from Humboldt Bay to the town of Crannell. Today it represents a beautiful, well-used segment of the California Coastal Trail.

Start at the southern trailhead, close to the Mad River Bridge. You cross the river on a 1942 steel truss bridge, which replaced a wooden, covered bridge built by Dolbeer and Carson Lumber Co. in 1905. The current bridge was brought in from Coos Bay.

The bridge crest provides a magnificent overlook of the Mad River, where you are likely to see marine wildlife like seals and sea otters. Many bird species, including cormorants, grebes, herons, ducks and the Aleutian goose (endangered until recently) also frequent the area.

Bluff-top views of the Pacific Ocean and ample bird-watching opportunities are particular draws of the popular Hammond Coastal Trail.

Location
Humboldt County

Endpoints
Clam Beach County Park to Mad River Bridge

Mileage
5.5

Roughness Index
2

Surface
Asphalt, dirt

67

Hammond Coastal Trail

rails·to·trails
conservancy

FINISH

P Clam Beach

Clam Beach Dr

Clam Beach Rd

Woody Rd

Baird Rd

Access Rd

Arcata Airport

Grange Rd

P

Airport Rd

Access Rd

Dows Prairie Rd

Hooven Rd

Central Ave

P

Half Way Ave

Barnett Ave

Norton Rd

Eagle Ln

PACIFIC OCEAN

Murray Rd

Boller Ave

McKinleyville

Bates Rd

Babler Rd

Redwood Hwy

Railroad Ave

Pickett Rd

Mckinleyville Ave

Hiller Rd

Holly Dr

2nd St

1st St

220

A St

B Ave

Ocean Dr

Bird Ave

Anderson Rd

Salmon Ave

School Rd

Colville

Sutter Rd

P 🚻

Azalea Ave

Cochran Rd

Birch Ave

START

Mad River Rd

Silva Rd

Bank Rd

220

N

0   0.25   0.5   1 Miles

Directly beyond the river you enter a bottoms habitat—sub-sea level agriculture and grazing land partially protected by the coastal dune lands to the west. You ascend a short but steep hill into the western fringe of McKinleyville, an unincorporated town of 13,000. Stop by Roger's Market for a cool drink and some fresh, locally picked mushrooms before heading to Hiller Park for some extra hiking and a restroom break.

Beyond the park the trail tunnels through a beautiful thick overgrowth of flora before opening up to spectacular bluffside views of the Pacific Ocean. Take a seat on a bench or continue on to the newest segment of the Hammond Trail, a paved section fusing the once separated northern and southern sections into one dream ride. This new roadside section shares traffic with Murray Rd. for about a quarter mile before turning toward Widow White Creek and a beautiful dune loop footpath.

The Hammond Coastal Trail north of Widow White Creek boasts more spectacular bluff overlooks before descending a steep gravel grade to sea level. Less advanced riders typically walk this section, which allows plenty of room for other bikers to pass. A short, smooth section crosses Strawberry Creek just before the trail terminates at Clam Beach County Park. Turn around and ride back to the bridge or arrange to be picked up. The trail can be ridden every day of the year, although the area often experiences rain in the winter months.

DIRECTIONS

To reach the southern trailhead, take Highway 101 to the CA 200/Central Avenue/Turner Road exit in McKinleyville. Make a slight left after exiting onto CA-200/Central Avene. Continue for 1.1 miles, and turn left (west) onto School Road. After 1 mile, turn left on Fischer Road and follow signs to Mad River Beach for 0.2 mile. The parking lot is on the left.

To reach the northern trailhead, take Highway 101 to the North Central Avenue exit north of McKinleyville. Continue for 0.2 mile, and turn left onto Central Avenue. Continue for about 200 feet on Clam Beach Drive. A parking lot is at the end of the road.

Contact: Humboldt County Parks
1106 2nd Street
Eureka, CA 95501
(707) 445-7651
www.redwoods.info/showrecord.asp?id=1600

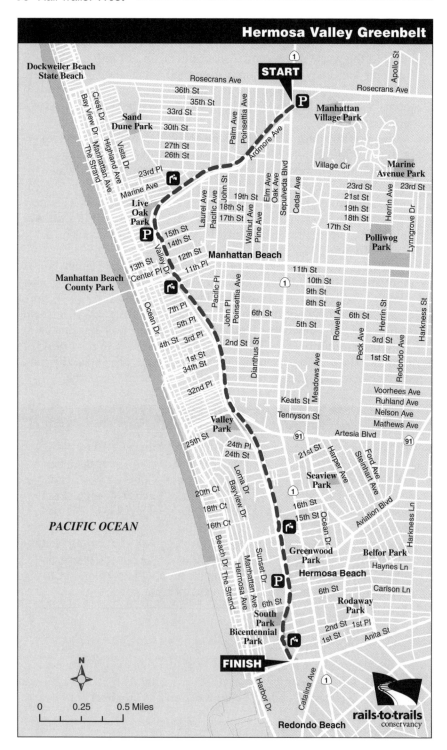

Hermosa Valley Greenbelt

Hermosa Valley Greenbelt

In the hustle and bustle of the greater Los Angeles area, the Hermosa Valley Greenbelt provides a cool, peaceful escape that is just minutes from the beach. This 3.5-mile pedestrian-only trail nestled in a greenway of lush vegetation and flowers seems almost hidden as it meanders through the oceanside suburbs of Manhattan Beach and Hermosa Beach. These communities, about 20 minutes south of Los Angeles, have all the quintessential qualities of classic Southern California towns, including palm-tree-lined boulevards and an assortment of surf shops, beachfront bars and restaurants.

Snug in the heart of Manhattan Beach, the Hermosa Valley Greenbelt serves as a linear park for the many locals enjoy its pedestrian-only pathway.

The northern end of the Hermosa Valley Greenbelt starts by a large parking lot off Rosecrans Avenue in Manhattan Beach and heads due south. The trail surface, like that of many trails in Southern California, is primarily woodchips. There are numerous road crossings all along the trail, so use caution.

As you begin, you are quickly surrounded by greenery. After passing through a tranquil Manhattan Beach neighborhood, you reach Live Oak Park where there are ball fields and picnic areas. Looking off to the right, you can see a distant hillside lined with gorgeous homes and, just beyond it, the Pacific Ocean. Continuing south, it becomes more obvious that the trail runs between two roads, North Admore Avenue to the west and North Valley Drive to the east. Both cities have landscaped the trail beautifully to make the roads as unobtrusive as possible.

Location
Los Angeles County

Endpoints
Redondo Beach to Manhattan Beach

Mileage
3.5

Roughness Index
2

Surface
Woodchips, dirt

As the trail crosses into the city of Hermosa Beach, you will find yourself on a gentle downhill slope. Throughout Hermosa Beach, the trail is surrounded by pleasant, quiet neighborhoods.

Near the home stretch of the trail, you cross Pier Avenue in Hermosa Beach. Just 200 yards down this street (right or left), you'll find a wide variety of restaurants and shops that overlook the Pacific Ocean. You will also find the expansive beaches that this community has to offer. The trail comes to an end at the intersection of Herondo Street and Valley Drive at the border of the town of Redondo Beach.

DIRECTIONS

To reach the northern trailhead, from Interstate 405 in Manhattan Beach, take the Rosecrans Avenue exit. Head (right or left) west on Rosecrans Avenue for 1.5 miles to a point just before its intersection with Sepulveda Boulevard. Turn left (south) into the large parking area that serves both the trailhead and the large shopping center on Rosecrans Avenue. The lot stretches toward the trailhead, which is opposite the shopping center at the far south end and is well signed.

To reach the southern trailhead, from I-405, take the 190th Street exit and follow 190th west (it becomes Herondo Street) for 4.8 miles. The trail is on the right (north) at the intersection of Herondo Street and Valley Drive. There is no good parking at the southern endpoint, but there is street parking in the surrounding neighborhoods.

Contact: Friends of the Parks
710 Pier Avenue
Hermosa Beach, CA 90254
www.hbfop.org

Iron Horse Regional Trail

The area surrounding the Iron Horse Regional Trail has an important history as part of the San Ramon Valley's agricultural and ranching past. Today, the Iron Horse Trail connects two counties and twelve cities, and runs through quiet residential neighborhoods, lively business and commercial districts, and shady greenbelts. This popular and extensively used trail roughly follows Interstate 680, beginning in the city of Concord on its northern end, and passing through Pleasant Hill, Walnut Creek, Alamo, Danville, San Ramon and Dublin before ending at the Dublin/Pleasanton BART station. Plans call for the trail to be extended on the north end to Suisun Bay in Martinez, and on the south end to Stanley Boulevard in Pleasanton, where an existing bike trail leads west to Livermore. This southern extension is well underway, with a 1-mile section midway between the BART station and Stanley Boulevard dedicated in March 2008.

At the northern end, the trail begins just south of Highway 4, near the northeast corner of Buchanan Airfield in Concord. The trail nears the Pleasant Hill BART station at about mile 5. A rest stop across the street from the BART parking lot features picnic tables, a drinking fountain and benches. The northernmost part of the trail, as well as the proposed area around Suisun Bay, follows a marshy area, which is a haven for ducks and geese. Continuing south, the area becomes increasingly more urban, as the trail passes nearby downtown Walnut Creek. (The Walnut Creek BART station is about a half mile off the trail). A bike overpass bridge spans Ignacio Avenue in a congested section of Walnut Creek. South of Walnut Creek the trail passes under Interstate 680 at Rudgear Road to the west side of the freeway. A staging area here features parking, a drinking fountain, benches and tables.

From this point the trail meanders through residential areas, where the presence of many "doggy bag stations" testifies to the popularity of the trail among local residents. The trail crosses residential streets numerous

Location
Alameda and Contra Costa counties

Endpoints
Near Buchanan Airfield in Concord to Dublin/Pleasanton BART station

Mileage
24.5

Roughness Index
1

Surface
Asphalt

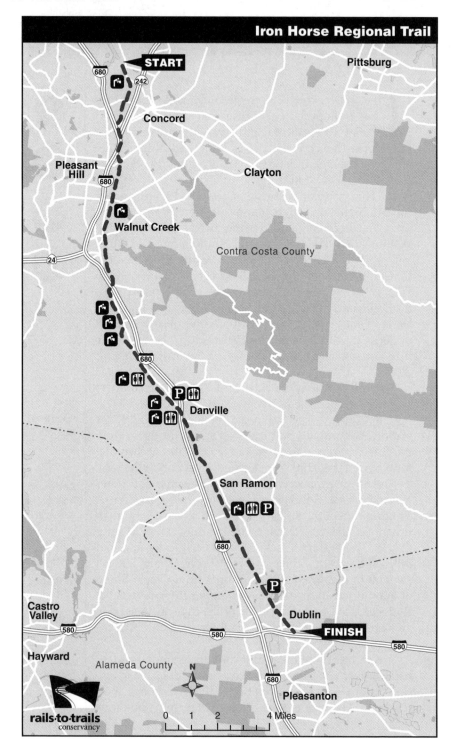

Iron Horse Regional Trail

times, typically in low traffic areas, and offers easy access to restaurants and shopping. Much of the trail in this section includes a dirt running path adjacent to the asphalt bike trail. In Danville, the trail passes directly behind the commercial downtown area. Nearby at the corner of Railroad and Prospect Avenues is the old Southern Pacific Depot, which is the only original depot remaining on the line. Just past the depot is a pleasant area featuring restaurants with outdoor seating overlooking the trail.

Picking up the trail again, you cross under I-680 to the east side and traverse Bishop Ranch Business Park, a commercial section that parallels the trail for about 2 miles. Next you reach the San Ramon Golf Club. The trail bisects the golf course, with chain-link fencing providing protection from errant golf balls. As the trail slices through Dublin, the environment is urban once more. The southern endpoint is at the BART parking lot on the Dublin side of the Dublin/Pleasanton BART station.

DIRECTIONS

To reach the northern trailhead, exit Highway 4 westbound at Arnold Industrial Way. Turn left onto Arnold Industrial Place and left again on Solano Way. Follow Solano Way as it crosses under Highway 4. Turn right onto Marsh Drive. The signed trailhead is on your left. Street parking is very limited.

To reach the southern trailhead, exit Interstate 580 at Hopyard Road. Turn right on Hopyard Road and proceed for 0.3 mile. Turn right on Dublin Boulevard and go 0.5 mile. Turn right on Demarcus Boulevard, which leads to the Dublin/Pleasanton BART station. The signed trailhead is at the north end of the parking lot.

Contact: East Bay Regional Parks District
2950 Peralta Oaks Court
P.O. Box 5381
Oakland, CA 94605
(888) EBPARKS (888-327-2757)
www.ebparks.org/parks/trails/iron_horse

Juanita Cooke Greenbelt

Parkwood Ave

90

Imperial Hwy

Chettenham Lane

Cienaga Dr

Walnut St

Montwood Park

Las Riendas Dr

Sandlewood Ave

Kirkwood Ln

Egerer Pl

Honeywood Ln

Dorwood Ave

Las Palmas Dr

START P

Hermosa Dr

Hermosa School Park

Country Hills Dr

Laguna Lake

Santa Maria Ave

Arbol Dr

Sunnywood Dr

La Travesia Dr

Clarion Dr

Coronado Dr

San Juan Park

Laguna Lake Park

N Harbor Blvd

West Coyote Hills Nature Park

Laguna Rd

Catalina Rd

Atherton Cir

(see page 41)

Terraza Pl

72

Parks Rd

Mesa Verde

Manzanita Dr

Bud Turner Trail

Verona Dr

Jose Way

Virgil Grissom Park

Yucca Ave

Roger Chaffee Park

Conejo Ln

Domingo Rd

N Euclid St

Bastanchury Rd

Green Acre Dr

Brea Dam Recreation Area

Domingo Rd

Simpson Park

W Valencia Mesa Dr

Parks Rd

Rodeo Rd

Sunnycrest Dr

Marelen Dr

Crestview Dr

Avolencia Dr

Highland Ave

Brea Blvd

Hiltscher Park

Richman Ave

El Dorado Dr

Hillcrest Park

N Berkeley Ave

Valley View Dr

Valley View Dr

Fern Dr

N

Fern Dr

Arroyo Dr

0   0.2   0.4 Miles

FINISH

rails·to·trails
conservancy

Union Ave

Juanita Cooke Greenbelt

The Juanita Cooke Greenbelt is a wonderful escape from the often-busy streets and highways of Orange County. This 2.5-mile trail in Fullerton connects some of the area's quiet neighborhoods with the downtown area, making it a great commuter path as well. The wide mulch and dirt surface makes this trail ideal for equestrian, pedestrian and bike use alike.

The trail is named for Juanita Cooke, who once served as a liaison for the Fullerton Recreational Riders, a local equestrian group that helped get the trail built. A plaque posted at West Valley View Drive gives the history of the trail. (Also posted at this location is the route of a 12-mile mountain bike ride around Fullerton.) Yet another trail, the Bud Turner Trail (page 41), named for another Fullerton Recreation Riders leader influential in making a trail a reality, connects to the greenbelt. Together, these two trails provide a refreshing space for all trail enthusiasts.

The Juanita Cooke Greenbelt with its excellent access to neighborhoods, parks and business is equal parts fun recreation and pleasant commuter trail.

Location
Orange County

Endpoints
Chettenham Lane to North Berkeley Avenue

Mileage
2.5

Roughness Index
1

Surface
Woodchips, dirt

Setting out from the northern trailhead at Laguna Lake Park, you will pass through some established neighborhoods. The scents provided by the flowering shrubs, citrus trees and the rest of the surrounding lush vegetation is a delightful bonus. As the trail approaches bustling downtown Fullerton, it crosses high above an active railroad corridor.

When you reach Laguna Road and the trail appears to come to an abrupt stop, cross the road and follow Morelia Place (directly across the street from the trail) for a few hundred yards of on-road travel. At the intersection of West Bastanchury Boulevard, cross this busy street and pick up the mulch and dirt trail once again on the other side. The last stretch of the trail is especially wide. Neighbors on both sides of the trail have put in beautiful landscaping, including lush gardens and high palms. Near Harbor Boulevard, very close to downtown Fullerton, the trail ends. Just to the left of the trail endpoint is a large Orange County courts parking area that can also be used by trail-goers.

Although the trail's official north end is at Hermosa Drive near Laguna Lake, the path continues north until it is interrupted by the Coyote Creek channel. A rough informal path goes as far north as Imperial Highway, where the railroad spur still exists and there is a signalized grade crossing.

DIRECTIONS

To reach the Laguna Lake Park endpoint, from Highway 91 (the Riverside Freeway) in Fullerton, take the Euclid Street exit. Head north on Euclid Street for about 4 miles to Lakeview Road. Turn right (east) on Lakeview Road and go 0.5 mile to Hermosa Drive. Turn right (east) on Hermosa Drive and go 0.1 mile to Lakeside Drive. The northwest entrance to Laguna Lake Park is at this intersection.

To reach the North County Court municipal building endpoint, from the Riverside Freeway, take exit 28 and head north on South Harbor Boulevard. Continue until you reach the intersection of North Berkeley Avenue. Take a left on North Berkeley Avenue, and the trailhead and parking area is at the North County Court Building immediately on your left.

Contact: Orange County Transportation Authority
550 South Main Street
P.O. Box 14184
Orange, CA 92868
(714) 636-RIDE (7433)
www.octa.net

Lafayette-Moraga Trail

T he 7.7-mile, suburban Lafayette-Moraga Trail traverses scenic green spaces and can be combined with a larger on-road network to form a loop known as the San Francisco Bay Trail. Be sure to make a note of the route on a trail map if your intention is to ride the rail-trail only—the most prominent signage describes the overall loop. When riding the on-road portion of the loop, you should have an understanding of operating a bicycle on a roadway.

Beginning at the north end, the trail passes through quiet neighborhoods. Mile markers are painted onto the trail surface, so you will always know how far you have been and how far you have left to enjoy. Approaching St. Mary's College, the views become more scenic; look for the college's cross statue off to the left and the American flag hilltop to the right.

The trail begins to feel more urban around mile 6 as it approaches and passes through Moraga. At the

The Lafayette-Moraga Trail is one of California's earliest rail-trails and was once a route for transporting timber from Oakland to Sacramento.

Location
Contra Costa County

Endpoints
Olympic Boulevard in Lafayette to East Bay Municipal Utility District's Valle Vista staging area

Mileage
7.7

Roughness Index
1

Surface
Asphalt, concrete

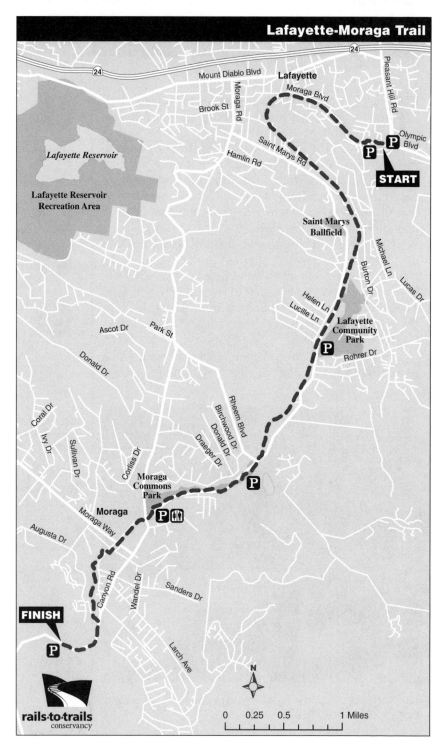

Lafayette-Moraga Trail

southern trail end, there are numerous hiking-only trails as part of the East Bay Municipal Utility District's Valle Vista staging area. A separate permit is required to use these trails. There are several parking lot areas and trailhead facilities along St. Mary's Road in addition to the trailheads at both ends; they include the Lafayette Community Center and Moraga Commons.

One of California's first rail-trails, this route was once used to move timber by mule, and later by steam locomotive, between Oakland and Sacramento. After the railroad venture was abandoned, the corridor was purchased for use as a utility corridor. Through successful partnerships between multiple agencies and companies such as Pacific Gas and Electric Company, the cities of Moraga and Lafayette, the Central Contra Costa Sanitary District and the East Bay Municipal Utility District, the 60-foot-wide corridor now adds tremendous value to trail users by connecting many points of interests and community assets.

Be sure to have someone in your party be assigned to "Hello Duty" because folks on this trail are friendly and are clearly out to enjoy the close to home proximity and beautiful scenery this trail has to offer. If hiking, be sure to get your permit and enjoy the hiking-only trails that are part of the Valle Vista staging area.

DIRECTIONS

From Oakland to the north end of the trail, take Highway 24 East towards Lafayette. Exit at Pleasant Hill Road and head south. Turn right (west) onto Olympic Boulevard, and the trailhead will be immediately on your right hand side (north).

From San Ramon to the north end, take Interstate 680 North and then take Highway 24 West. Exit at Pleasant Hill Road and head south. Turn right (west) onto Olympic Boulevard and the trailhead will be immediately on your right hand side (north).

Contact: East Bay Regional Park District
2950 Peralta Oaks Court
Oakland, CA 94605
(925) 687-3419
www.ebparks.org

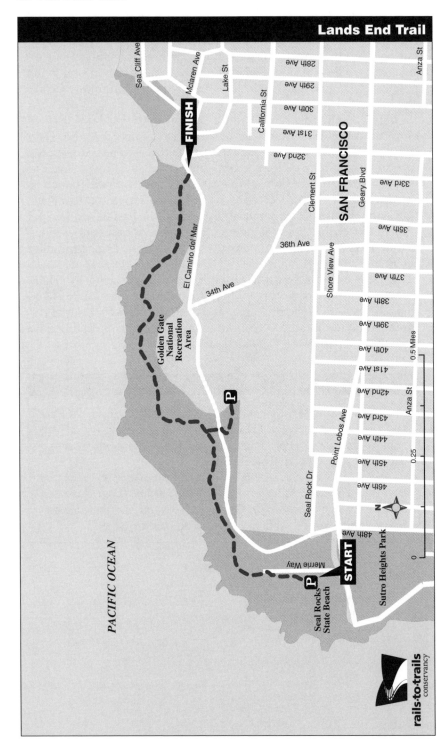

Lands End Trail

Riding high on the cliffs at North America's western edge, this San Francisco area trail offers unbeatable views of the Golden Gate Bridge and the Pacific Ocean at San Francisco Bay. Add to that a chance to see old shipwrecks, historical monuments, marine animals and birds (cormorants and oystercatchers, among others), and such San Francisco landmarks as the Cliff House, Sutro Baths and the Palace of the Legion of Honor, and you have the makings of a rich rail-trail experience. Be sure to bring your camera, and stop off at the several vista points (half-circle rest areas on the oceanside of the trail).

Lands End Trail has a colorful history. Gustav Sutro forged the corridor in 1888 as part of the Park and Cliff House Railway, to bring San Franciscans from downtown out to the Cliff House resort and Sutro Baths that his brother, mining magnate Adolph Sutro, was building on the rugged San Francisco coast. For just 5 cents,

The Lands End Trail winds along San Francisco's cliff-top coastline, combining a typical rail-trail with extending footpaths and gasp-worthy Pacific Ocean views.

Location
San Francisco County

Endpoints
Merrie Way parking lot to El Camino del Mar

Mileage
2

Roughness Index
2

Surface
Crushed stone, dirt

passengers could enjoy a ride around Lands End in the railroad's open-air carriages. Today, the Cliff House, Sutro Bath and Lands End area are all part of the Golden Gate National Recreation Area, one of the largest urban national parks in the world.

Only the ruins of the once grand Sutro Baths remain, and you can walk downhill (toward the coast) on a side path from the north side of the Merrie Way parking lot to see them. The Cliff House, the third building with that name on this spot, is an elegant place for a drink or meal with wonderful ocean views and is a short walk from the Merrie Way parking lot; just head west (downhill) on Point Lobos Avenue about a quarter mile.

If you start from the Merrie Way parking lot, you'll see the Lands End trailhead at the north end of the lot. You wind up a slight hill, past the newly restored sections of trail where the Golden Gate National Park staff and volunteers have restored native vegetation along the trail route and thinned the cypress forest to open up views of the coast, and of the rocky shores that have claimed more than a few unlucky ships. From the trail you can see remains of three shipwrecks dating from the 1920s and '30s. The year 1937 was particularly unforgiving: Both the passenger ship *Frank Buck* and the freighter *Ohioan* were pierced by the same rocky outcroppings. In 1922 the *Lyman Stewart* went down in the same area. (From the northwest vista point at the bottom of the stairs to the *USS San Francisco* memorial parking lot, look over the edge—at low tide, you can spot the sternpost and boilers of the *Ohioan*).

For remains of the other two shipwrecks, look carefully from the trail between the northwest vista point and the eastern end of the trail. The middle stretch of the trail provides the best vantage point for viewing the Golden Gate Bridge and the Marin Headlands on the north side of the bridge. If you want to visit the Palace of the Legion of Honor, keep an eye out for a staircase heading uphill on the right, about two-thirds of a mile from your starting point at Merrie Way parking lot.

The Palace of the Legion of Honor, a beautiful Beaux Arts building erected in 1921 to honor California soldiers who died in World War I, contains a highly regarded art collection, ranging from ancient pieces to European treasures, including a monumental cast of Rodin's *Thinker*. Standing outside the building you can enjoy great views of the Golden Gate Bridge and the city of San Francisco.

If you don't want to detour to the Palace of the Legion of Honor, then pass by the stairs leading to the museum parking lot, and stay on the trail, which is labeled as the COASTAL TRAIL, for another 1.3 miles of great bridge and coastal views. The trail ends where it intersects with El Camino del Mar near 33rd Avenue. To make this a loop rather than an up-and-back, you can pick up the El Camino del Mar Trail from the Palace of the Legion of Honor overlook; it leads back to the memorial parking lot and the intersection with the Lands End Trail.

Be careful to stay on the trail in the Lands End area, as the cliffs are steep and slippery. The trail surface varies but is smooth, decomposed granite for about the first two-thirds of a mile from Merrie Way, and then becomes a dirt trail. There are stairs to navigate about halfway through, and bikes are not allowed through this section.

DIRECTIONS

There are multiple access points along the Lands End Trail.

The western trailhead at Merrie Way parking lot is wheelchair accessible. From downtown San Francisco, take Geary Boulevard west about 5 miles. At 41st Avenue stay right as Geary splits and becomes Point Lobos Avenue. About 500 feet past 48th Avenue, turn right (north) into the Merrie Way parking lot, where there is ample parking.

To reach the USS *San Francisco* memorial parking lot, follow the directions as above, but at 48th Avenue, turn right (north) on El Camino del Mar to the memorial parking lot, from which you follow stairs to the trail.

To reach the El Camino del Mar trailhead, take Geary Boulevard to 32nd Avenue and turn right. Drive several blocks and make a left on El Camino del Mar. Park on the street.

Contact: Golden Gate National Parks
Golden Gate National Parks Building 201
Fort Mason
San Francisco, CA 94123
(415) 561-4700
www.parksconservancy.org/visit/park.asp?pageKey=104

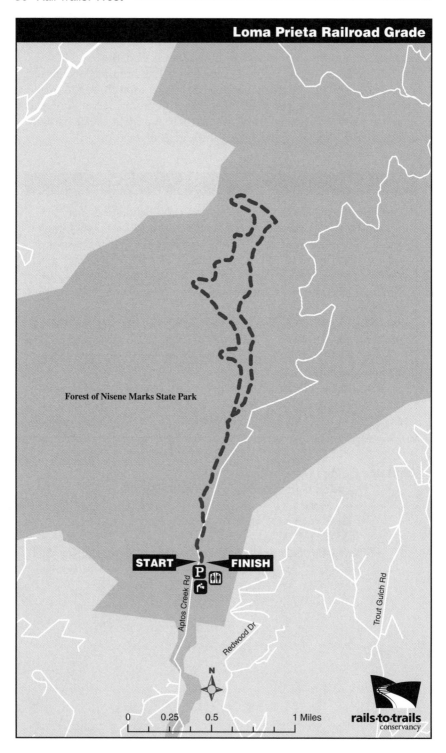

Loma Prieta Railroad Grade

Forest of Nisene Marks State Park

START FINISH

Aptos Creek Rd

Redwood Dr

Trout Gulch Rd

N

0   0.25   0.5   1 Miles

rails·to·trails
conservancy

Loma Prieta Railroad Grade

This extremely scenic rail-trail is located in the majestic Forest of Nisene Marks State Park near Aptos, Calif. The park was the site of major logging operations by the Loma Prieta Lumber Company from 1883 until 1923. In the 1950s, Herman, Agnes and Andrew Marks purchased about 9,700 acres of this land, thinking the area to be rich in oil. When exploration did not produce oil, the Marks family deeded the property in 1963 to the state in honor of their mother, Nisene Marks. The deed specified that the forest must not be developed, allowing the natural regeneration process to continue. Today Nisene Marks State Park thrives, with 30 miles of hiking trails, several campsites and multiple picnic areas. The evergreens, oaks, bays and madrones that were so extensively logged years ago are now abundant throughout the park.

From the Porter Family Picnic Area, you walk along a paved road for about a quarter mile to the trailhead for

Like many logging loop trails, the Loma Prieta Railroad Grade follows the railroad grade for some of its length as well old forest road routes.

Location
Santa Cruz County

Endpoints
Porter Family Picnic Area in the Forest of Nisene Marks State Park

Mileage
5.5

Roughness Index
2

Surface
Dirt

the Loma Prieta Grade Trail. As you turn left onto the trail, you begin ascending into the woods, with views of lovely Bridge Creek, until you reach the Porter House historic site, which was once the home of Warren Porter, former secretary for the Loma Prieta Lumber Company.

Continue along the path until you reach a junction with Bridge Creek Trail. This junction marks the start of a loop trail; you can go either direction from here. If you veer left, you soon come to Hoffman Historic Site, the remains of a logging camp that operated between 1918 and 1921. You can still see a scattering of ties, cables and trestle timbers here.

Beyond the camp you come to an intersection with Big Stump Gap Trail. Remain on the rail-trail here as it continues north and then makes a sharp right turn. You will pass Bridge Creek Historic Site, another historic logging camp. A short side trail here leads to Maple Falls, one of two waterfalls within Nisene Marks Park. The main trail continues through the redwoods, following the path of Bridge Creek and descending to rejoin the railroad grade at the Porter House.

There are restrooms and water fountains at the parking lot. The trail is shaded, but it's a good idea to bring along plenty of water. Several benches along the walk make inviting places to rest and have lunch. Neither dogs nor bicycles are allowed on the trail.

DIRECTIONS

From Highway 1 in Aptos take the State Park Drive exit to Soquel Drive. Turn right (east) on Soquel Drive and continue about a mile to the intersection with Aptos Creek Road. Turn left on Aptos Creek Road and go a half mile to the Forest of Nisene Marks State Park entrance station. Continue another 4 miles to the Porter Family Picnic Area parking lot. The signed trailhead is visible from the parking lot.

Contact: California State Parks
Soquel Drive
Aptos, CA 95003
(831) 763-7062
www.parks.ca.gov/?page_id=666

Los Gatos Creek Trail

It is difficult to travel through suburban Los Gatos for more than a few minutes without noticing an abundance of cyclists and runners in the area. If you are strolling downtown, chances are that the biker whizzing by you is headed for the Los Gatos Creek Trail. During the week this rail-trail sees a moderate amount of traffic, but on weekends it bustles with activity. From 20-somethings clutching their morning lattes to energetic cyclists and families walking their dogs, you'll see everyone out enjoying this path on Saturdays and Sundays.

In its entirety, the Los Gatos Creek Trail spans 9.7 miles and passes through several cities, but this description focuses on the Los Gatos portion that is a rail-trail. It follows a former South Pacific Coast Railroad line that transported passengers from Santa Cruz to Alameda in the late 1800s. Begin at the northern end next to the landmark Forbes Mill Museum, an 1854 flour mill and annex

The Los Gatos Creek Trail serves as a siren's call on weekends when all manner of trail users are out enjoying the pathway.

Location
Santa Clara County

Endpoints
Forbes Mill Museum to Lexington Reservoir

Mileage
1.8

Roughness Index
3

Surface
Dirt, gravel

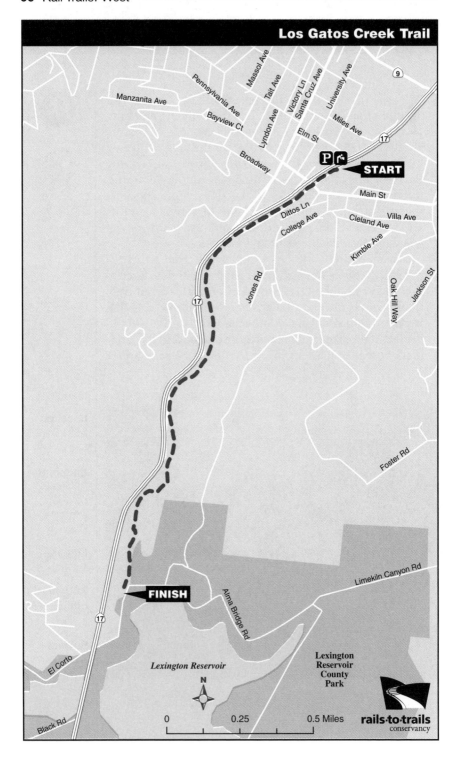

Los Gatos Creek Trail

that exhibits Los Gatos area memorabilia. You will find a water fountain there—the only one on the trail—but no restrooms.

Los Gatos Creek is on your left as you step onto the unpaved trail. Wrapped in riparian undergrowth, the sparkling creek is lovely. A not-so-bucolic feature, Highway 17, is on your right, but the creek effectively masks the sound of the nearby traffic. The trail has a moderate incline as it flows northward, and includes one short but steep climb at 1.3 miles. The surface is a bit rocky here, and only experienced cyclists will be able to ascend it without dismounting.

After this incline the trail levels off and continues flat toward a paved footbridge. This is technically the end of the trail, and most runners turn back here. If you wish to continue, cross this bridge and head up a steep, paved switchback, which brings you to Alma Bridge Road. Just across Alma Bridge Road is Lexington Reservoir County Park, a lovely daytime destination. Its main attraction is the 914-acre human-made Lexington Reservoir for which the park is named. The park offers nonmotorized boating, fishing, hiking trails and ample areas to picnic.

DIRECTIONS

To reach the northern trailhead, from Highway 17, exit at East Los Gatos Avenue and turn right on Los Gatos-Saratoga Road. Continue on this road until it becomes East Main Street. Turn right on Church Street, which will take you straight into the Forbes Mill parking lot. The signed trailhead is located next to the Forbes Mill Museum.

Contact: Department of Parks and Recreation
Santa Clara County
1250 Dell Avenue
Campbell, CA 95008
(408) 535-3570
www.sjparks.org/Trails/LosGatos/LosGatos.asp

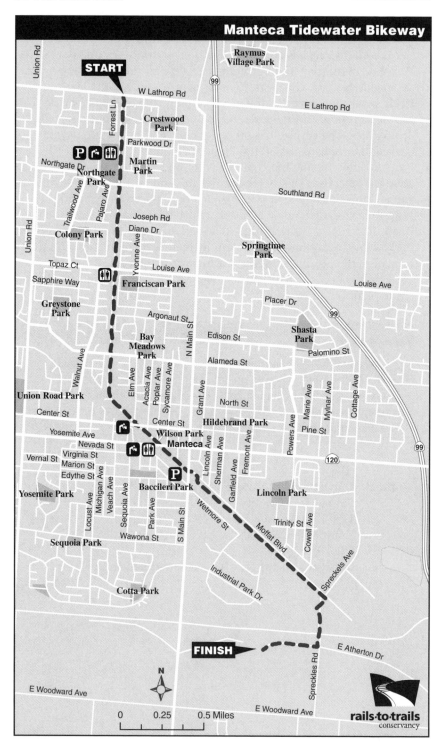

Manteca Tidewater Bikeway

START

Union Rd

Raymus Village Park

W Lathrop Rd

E Lathrop Rd

99

Forrest Ln

Crestwood Park

Parkwood Dr

P

Northgate Dr

Northgate Park

Martin Park

Southland Rd

Trailwood Ave

Pajaro Ave

Colony Park

Joseph Rd

Diane Dr

Union Rd

Yvonne Ave

Louise Ave

Springtime Park

Topaz Ct

Sapphire Way

Franciscan Park

Louise Ave

Greystone Park

Argonaut St

N Main St

Placer Dr

99

Shasta Park

Walnut Ave

Bay Meadows Park

Edison St

Palomino St

Alameda St

Union Road Park

Center St

Elm Ave

Acacia Ave

Poplar Ave

Sycamore Ave

Grant Ave

North St

Cottage Ave

Marie Ave

Mylnar Ave

Hildebrand Park

Powers Ave

Pine St

Yosemite Ave

Wilson Park

Nevada St

Manteca

Vernal St

Virginia St

Marion St

Edythe St

Michigan Ave

Veach Ave

Locust Ave

Sequoia Ave

Park Ave

S Main St

P

Baccileri Park

Lincoln Ave

Sherman Ave

Garfield Ave

Fremont Ave

99

120

Lincoln Park

Yosemite Park

Wawona St

Wetmore St

Moffat Blvd

Trinity St

Cowell Ave

Sequoia Park

Cotta Park

Industrial Park Dr

Spreckels Ave

FINISH

E Atherton Dr

Spreckles Rd

N

E Woodward Ave

E Woodward Ave

0   0.25   0.5 Miles

rails·to·trails
conservancy

Manteca Tidewater Bikeway

The Manteca Tidewater Bikeway is a 4-mile multi-use trail running north to south through the city of Manteca, Calif. The flat asphalt corridor is up to 100 feet wide in places and is popular with bikers, skaters and walkers. There is also an adjacent 4-foot-wide crushed gravel path for runners. This pleasant urban trail connects neighborhoods on the city's southern and northern boundaries to the central business section. It also connects to various parks, including Library Park and a sports and skateboard park.The recently renovated Library Park features a large fountain; new facilities, including recreational fields and a gazebo; and several murals highlighting important historical aspects of Manteca's culture and history. One of the best murals tells the story of the Yokut Indian tribe, the earliest known residents in the area.

The trail follows the path of the old Tidewater Railway, an interurban passenger and freight rail. Today,

With a fountain, skateboard park, gazebo and recreation fields along its path, the Manteca Tidewater Bikeway is an award-winning community transportation playground.

Location
San Joaquin County

Endpoints
West Lathrop Road to East Atherton Drive

Mileage
4

Roughness Index
1

Surface
Asphalt

parts of the line that still run are operated by Union Pacific, and the former Tidewater Southern Railway has one of highest percentages of interurban rail still running. The trail begins at West Lathrop Road on the north end of the city. You pass through a quiet, residential section before reaching the city sports and skateboard park, a little more than halfway through the trail. Near the skate park the trail enters downtown Manteca. From here you cross through the town, with industrial buildings on both sides. An active railroad line shares the corridor until it ends at another residential area at the southern end of the city.

In 2001, the Manteca Tidewater Bikeway was one of seven recipients of a Project Award at the TRANNY Awards, which are sponsored by the California Transportation Foundation, a nonprofit organization dedicated to recognizing outstanding transportation performance and achievement.

DIRECTIONS

To reach the northern trailhead, exit Highway 99 at East Lathrop Road and go 0.5 mile. The trailhead will be on your right. Parking is not permitted on this busy street, but there is a church parking lot across the street.

To reach the southern trailhead, exit Highway 120 at South Main Street. Turn left and proceed 0.4 mile to East Woodward Avenue. Turn right on Woodward and go 0.9 mile to Spreckles Road. Turn left on Spreckles Road, turn left on East Atherton Drive, and follow it until it ends. There is no parking in this residential area.

Contact: Parks and Recreation Department
City of Manteca
1001 West Center Street
Manteca, CA 95337
(209) 239-8470
www.ci.manteca.ca.us/PARKS

Martin Luther King Promenade

Running through downtown San Diego, the Martin Luther King Promenade is a vibrant, palm-lined ribbon that parallels an active trolley line along Harbor Drive. The trail provides direct access to many of the city's highlights, and its rich supply of public art, grassy areas, water fountains and people-watching opportunities makes the promenade a San Diego highlight in itself.

You'll want to start on the northern end of the trail, where there is ample parking in a lot on West Broadway across the street from the Santa Fe Depot. Built in 1915 in the classic Spanish mission and Colonial Revival style, the depot is a terminus of the nation's second-busiest Amtrak rail corridor, San Diego Northern's Coaster commuter route. Once at risk of being torn down and now widely celebrated, the historic depot is worth a visit before heading out on the trail. Listed in the National Register of Historic Places, the depot also houses the library of the San Diego Railroad Museum.

The Martin Luther King Promenade parallels a trolley line and is a San Diego highlight, perfect for a leisurely bike ride or stroll.

The trail begins just west of the active railroad tracks. Head south for an eighth of a mile, and follow the trail as it becomes a wide path weaving between two apartment buildings. After passing the buildings, turn left onto G Street, cross Kettner Boulevard, and reconnect with the off-street path on the south side of the street.

The wide variety of sights to take in along the trail makes it ideal for a leisurely bike ride or stroll. Just past Kettner Boulevard, a stand of San Diego's tall towers

Location
San Diego County

Endpoints
West Broadway to 8th Avenue and Harbor Drive

Mileage
1.1

Roughness Index
1

Surface
Asphalt

95

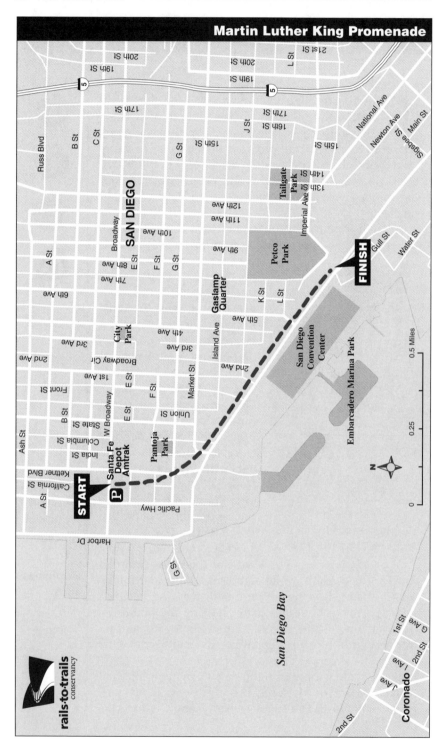

flanks the north side of the trail, opposite the San Diego Convention Center. At the 5th Avenue intersection, make a left to the entrance to the Gaslamp Quarter, with its seemingly endless offering of restaurants, shops, bars and historical charm. The Gaslamp, which contains more than 90 Victorian-era historic buildings, was revitalized in the 1980s and 1990s. Today it is a major San Diego destination for tourists and locals alike. Also nearby is Petco Park, home of the San Diego Padres.

The promenade ends at the intersection of 8th Avenue and Harbor Drive. Return the way you came.

DIRECTIONS

To reach the northern trailhead in downtown San Diego, from Harbor Drive, head east on West Broadway Avenue to the intersection with Pacific Highway. The Santa Fe Depot is located on West Broadway between Pacific Highway and Kettner Boulevard. The trailhead is across West Broadway from the depot, just west of the railroad tracks. Park in the lot next to the trailhead.

To reach the southern trailhead, head farther south on Harbor Drive to 8th Avenue to a small parking lot.

Contact: City of San Diego
1010 Second Avenue, Suite 800
San Diego, CA 92101
(619) 533-3126

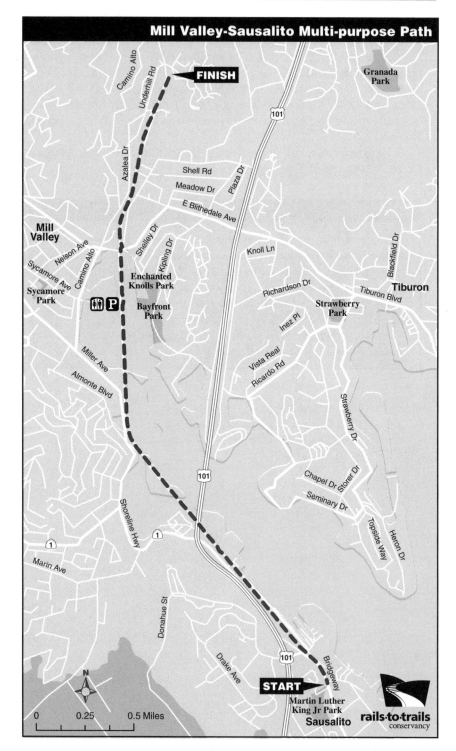

Mill Valley-Sausalito Multi-purpose Path

Camino Alto
Underhill Rd
← FINISH
Granada Park

101

Azalea Dr

Shell Rd
Meadow Dr
Plaza Dr
E Blithedale Ave

Mill Valley

Nelson Ave
Camino Alto
Shelley Dr
Kipling Dr
Knoll Ln

Blackfield Dr

Sycamore Ave
Sycamore Park
Enchanted Knolls Park
Richardson Dr
Strawberry Park
Tiburon Blvd
Tiburon

Bayfront Park
Inez Pl

Miller Ave
Vista Real
Ricardo Rd

Almonte Blvd
Strawberry Dr

101

Chapel Dr
Storer Dr
Seminary Dr

Shoreline Hwy
1
Topside Way
Heron Dr

1
Marin Ave

Donahue St

Drake Ave

101

Bridgeway

N

START
Martin Luther King Jr Park
Sausalito

0   0.25   0.5 Miles

rails·to·trails
conservancy

Mill Valley-Sausalito Multi-purpose Path

Mill Valley-Sausalito Multi-purpose Path is a convenient connection between neighborhoods, schools, shopping, restaurants and a skate park. There is also an adjacent dog park, Mill Valley Dog Park. Between the skate and dog parks, on a nice day there can be all kinds of excitement and an assortment of aerobatic displays by man and beast alike to enjoy.

The short dirt section at the north end is just a minor neighborhood connection and can easily be omitted if you are riding a bike or skating. Otherwise, the trail is mostly asphalt and turns to concrete as the trail approaches the southern end, which parallels a fairly busy roadway. Overall, the trail gets a good mix of cyclists, walkers, joggers and skaters, so brush up on the rules of the trails before you begin. You can also access the trail by way of the ferry in Sausalito, making it possible to connect with other opportunities in San Francisco and Marin County. You could even rent a bike in San

Whether you're there for parks for kids or parks for pets, the Mill Valley-Sausalito Multi-purpose Path and the amenities it links to are fun for the whole family.

Location
Marin County

Endpoints
North of Vasco Court in Mill Valley to Gate 5 Road in Sausalito

Mileage
3.5

Roughness Index
2

Surface
Asphalt, dirt, concrete

Francisco and take the ferry to Sausalito. This can make for a great day of exploring the region. Although the trail is rather short, it and the nearby shoreline and art galleries are all worth exploring.

The best feature of the trail is its views of the bay as it passes through a scenic open wetland marsh area. You will see many species of birds here, including the marsh wren, brown pelican, and maybe even a raptor if you are lucky. Be sure to enjoy the houseboats of Sausalito as you cruise by.

Parking is available at many of the adjoining business areas and at the Sycamore Avenue trailhead, where there is a public restroom.

DIRECTIONS

To reach the parking at Sycamore Avenue, take Highway 101 and exit at East Blithedale Avenue. Take East Blithedale Avenue west to Camino Alto and turn left (south). Take Camino Alto to Sycamore Avenue and turn left (east). Parking is available at the end of the road.

Contact: Marin County Department of Parks and Open Space
Marin County Civic Center, Room 415
3501 Civic Center Drive
San Rafael, CA 94903
(415) 499-6387
www.co.marin.ca.us/depts/pk/main/pos/
pdmultippath.cfm

Monterey Peninsula Recreational Trail

Winding along the coast of Monterey, Calif., the Monterey Peninsula Recreational Trail (also known as the Monterey Bay Coastal Trail) offers breathtaking views of the Pacific Ocean and a great way to tour the city while enjoying the outdoors. This wonderful coastal rail-trail currently extends 18 miles from Pacific Grove to Castroville, and is regarded as one of the most scenic long trails in California.

The trail follows the former Southern Pacific Railroad line, which was once used to transfer goods between the historic fishing town of Monterey and the rest of northen California. Beginning in Pacific Grove at the Lovers Point trailhead, you will want to take a picture of the beautiful rocky shoreline to the west. But don't put your camera away yet—the beautiful views continue and there are many photo opportunities along the trail of beach scenes, otters, boats, kayakers and more.

Curving around the shore of Monterey Bay, Monterey Peninsula Recreational Trail is magnificently scenic and offers recreation on and off the trail.

After 0.3 mile you come to a mural portraying the history of the area around the trail. About a mile from the trailhead, you reach Cannery Row. Made famous by John Steinbeck, this area offers many restaurants, as well as shopping, lodging and entertainment for all ages.

After a string of street crossings, you arrive at Monterey Bay Aquarium. Recognized as one of the best in the world, the aquarium exhibits a wide array of sea creatures, from a giant octopus to nearly two dozen species of sharks. Just beyond the aquarium, roughly 1.5 miles into the journey, you reach Fisherman's Shoreline Park

Location
Monterey County

Endpoints
Pacific Grove to Castroville

Mileage
18

Roughness Index
1

Surface
Asphalt

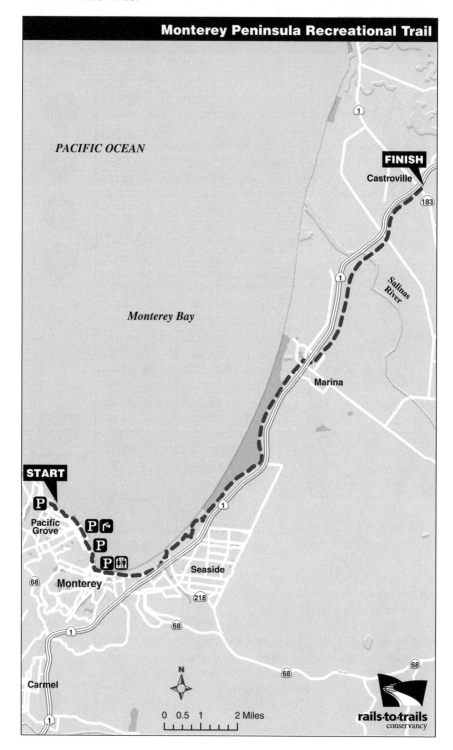

Monterey Peninsula Recreational Trail

PACIFIC OCEAN

FINISH

Castroville

183

1

Salinas River

Monterey Bay

Marina

START

P

Pacific Grove

P

P

P

Seaside

1

68

Monterey

218

1

68

Carmel

68

68

N

0 0.5 1   2 Miles

1

rails·to·trails
conservancy

and San Carlos Beach. San Carlos is a popular destination for diving, and you might see some shore divers preparing for an underwater adventure. The trail continues toward a smaller beach where you can view sailing and fishing boats scattered throughout the bay.

At the 2-mile mark you come to Fisherman's Wharf, with its restaurants, shops and great views of the ocean. The wharf is probably the most popular destination on the trail because of its location, scenery and historical displays, including several generations of fishing craft.

Beyond the wharf, the pathway runs close to the usually busy Del Monte Road. But the scene soon changes as you enter the northern end of the trail. You come to Monterey State Beach, with its impressive sand dunes and, farther down the trail, a eucalyptus forest that separates the trail from the road. The next few miles become a bit more commercial as the trail follows the coastline toward the shopping centers at Seaside, and a few more miles to the city of Marina. It's another 8 miles to the trail's end in Castroville. You can either ride back the way you came, or arrange a shuttle beforehand in Castroville.

DIRECTIONS

To reach the Pacific Grove trailhead, from Highway 1, take the Del Monte Avenue (402B) exit toward Pacific Grove. Travel 2 miles west on Del Monte Avenue, then veer right onto Lighthouse Avenue. Continue on Lighthouse Avenue for 1.4 miles, turn right on David Avenue and soon after turn left on Ocean View Boulevard. Continue for 1 mile to Jewell Avenue. The trailhead is near the corner of Ocean View Boulevard and Jewell Avenue. You can either park in the paid lot at the trailhead or look for street parking nearby.

To reach the Castroville trailhead, from Highway 1, take Highway 183, or Merritt Street east into Castroville. Turn right onto Haro Street. The bike path begins at the end of the street.

Contact: Monterey Peninsula Regional Park District
60 Garden Court, Suite 325
Monterey, California 93940
(831) 372-3196
www.mprpd.org

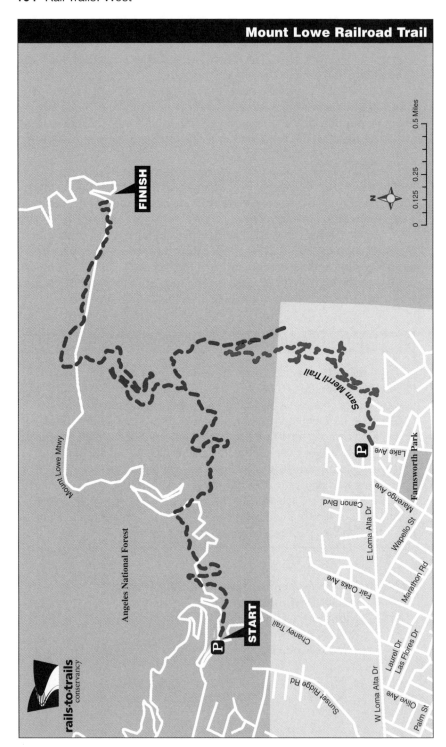

Mount Lowe Railroad Trail

Mount Lowe Railroad Trail

The Mount Lowe Railroad Trail is as unique and remarkable a trail as any you may travel. Many historic and informational signs along the path tell the story of the trail and the amazing rail line that once ascended the mountain. You can glean much information from these signs about Professor Thaddeus S.C. Lowe, the ballooning, fortunes he made and lost, the trail's mountaintop resort and Echo Mountain Railway buildings. The railroad had an Alpine Division and one 1915 photograph features a vertical rock bridge and a circular (a special track designed to rotate railcars) with a trolley on it. Back in present-day, you'll also see the smog of greater Los Angeles, but high above on the Mount Lowe Trail, it won't detract from the spectacular scenery around you.

Starting at the western trailhead on Chaney Trail, your adventure begins with a very steep, 2.35-mile climb up the mountain on a paved fire road to Sunset Ridge, elevation 2,133 feet. At this point you can either veer east for a 1-mile branch of the Mount Lowe Trail, ending at the Echo Mountain Railway buildings and a 2,000-foot drop-off, or continue north for approximately 2.5 miles to the ruins of the Mount Lowe lodge.

Heading east, the surface changes to dirt and gravel—some fist-size rocks—and the trail becomes a true hiking route. Along this remarkable bench-cut rail grade are numerous signs showing pictures of the train cars running along the tracks where you are now walking. It is truly an engineering marvel to imagine trainloads of people making the same trek. The last mile of this trail branch leads to the original purpose of the railroad, which was to get people and supplies to Mount Wilson where Professor Lowe built his resort. The foundations of the railway buildings are still very much intact and come to life with many interpretive panels. The relics of the old tramway that brought people to the lodge are also visible, including some huge iron gears, as well as coiled pieces of the massive cables that pulled the tram cars up the mountain.

Location
Los Angeles County

Endpoints
Chaney Trail to Chaney Trailhead

Mileage
5.8

Roughness Index
3

Surface
Dirt, asphalt, gravel

If instead of heading east, you continue north, the fire road soon gives way to its own gravel path, flattening out in rail-trail style but with some truly spine-tingling switchbacks as you climb higher and higher up the mountainside. Again, the views from high above the Los Angeles basin are stunning. As the trail nears the lodge ruins, the pathway transforms again into a more typical and undulating single-track hiking trail. At the lodge, be sure to read the interpretive signs that show pictures of how the lodge once appeared, complete with well-frocked visitors on the once resplendent veranda. Today, picnic tables among the pines serve as your dining area.

No matter which route you take, the Mount Lowe Railroad Trail delivers unbelievable panoramic views of Pasadena, the Pacific Ocean and countless other wonders that will inspire you as they did Professor Lowe nearly a century ago.

DIRECTIONS

To reach the eastern trailhead from Interstate 210, take the North Lake exit and follow North Lake Avenue for 3.6 miles to the junction of North Lake Avenue and East Loma Alta Drive. The Sam Merril Trail starts at the wrought iron gate and connects to the Mt. Lowe Railroad Trail.

To reach the western trailhead from I-210, take the North Lake exit and follow North Lake Avenue for 3.6 miles to the junction of North Lake Avenue and East Loma Alta Drive. Turn left on East Loma Alta Drive and follow it for 1 mile. Turn right on Chaney Trail, and follow it for 1.1 miles to the gated trailhead. To park there you must have a Forest Adventure Pass or Golden Passport (available at U.S. Forest Service District offices or sporting/biking stores) and must hang it on your rearview mirror.

Contact: Angeles National Forest
Supervisor's Office
701 North Santa Anita Avenue
Arcadia, CA 91006
(626) 574-5200
www.fs.fed.us/r5/angeles

Ohlone Greenway

Named for the Ohlone Indians who once lived in the area, this trail doubles as a commuting corridor and a recreation destination for the cities of Berkeley, Albany and El Cerrito. While the Ohlone Greenway is certainly an urban trail, it weaves together a number of parks and green spaces, community gardens and interpretive kiosks, to create a pleasurable and informative trail experience. The greenway's smooth asphalt surface makes it suitable for a variety of users.

The greenway begins at the east end of Ohlone Park in Berkeley, and runs westward. Soon after setting off you reach a leash-less dog park. Like a number of progressive ideas coming from Berkeley, this park was the first of its kind in the U.S. Beyond the dog park, the park opens up to a width of about 100 feet. This broad linear park hosts a number of attractions, including a playground, a community garden, exercise equipment, interactive public art and a variety of trees and foliage. This section of the trail gets quite a bit of traffic.

Ohlone Park at the trail's southern endpoint is just one of many trailside community greenspaces that enhance and characterize the urban Ohlone Greenway.

Location
Alameda and Contra Costa counties

Endpoints
Berkeley to El Cerrito

Mileage
5.3

Roughness Index
1

Surface
Asphalt

107

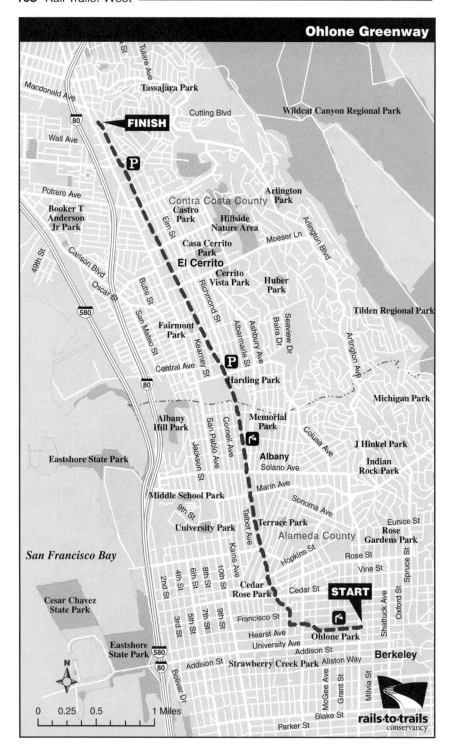

Ohlone Greenway

FINISH

Macdonald Ave
Tulare Ave
Tassajara Park
Cutting Blvd
Wildcat Canyon Regional Park
Wall Ave
80
P
Potrero Ave
Contra Costa County
Arlington Park
Booker T Anderson Jr Park
Castro Park
Hillside Nature Area
Elm St
Casa Cerrito Park
Moeser Ln
49th St
Carlson Blvd
El Cerrito
Cerrito Vista Park
Huber Park
Arlington Blvd
Oscar St
580
Richmond St
Butte St
Tilden Regional Park
Fairmont Park
Albemarle St
Ashbury Ave
Balra Dr
Seaview Dr
San Mateo St
Kearney St
Central Ave
Arlington Ave
80
P
Harding Park
Michigan Park
Albany Hill Park
Cornell Ave
San Pablo Ave
Memorial Park
Colusa Ave
J Hinkel Park
Eastshore State Park
Jackson St
Albany
Solano Ave
Indian Rock Park
Middle School Park
9th St
Marin Ave
Sonoma Ave
University Park
Talbot Ave
Terrace Park
Alameda County
Eunice St
Rose Gardens Park
San Francisco Bay
Kains Ave
Hopkins St
Rose St
Spruce St
Vine St
Oxford St
Shattuck St
10th St
8th St
6th St
4th St
2nd St
9th St
7th St
5th St
3rd St
Cedar Rose Park
Cedar St
START
Cesar Chavez State Park
Francisco St
Milvia St
Hearst Ave
Ohlone Park
Eastshore State Park
580
University Ave
Addison St
Berkeley
80
Addison St
Strawberry Creek Park
Allston Way
McGee Ave
Grant St
Blake St
N
Bolivar Dr
0   0.25   0.5   1 Miles
Parker St

rails·to·trails
conservancy

As the trail exits the park and crosses Sacramento Street near the North Berkeley BART station, it becomes an on-street bike path. Make a right on Acton Street and reconnect with the off-street path near the corner of Acton and Virginia streets. You'll pass a community garden and interpretive signs about the trail and the Ohlone people. For several miles after this point, you will be riding beside or underneath the elevated BART tracks. The trail, with separate cycling and walking paths in most sections, runs through the towns of Albany and El Cerrito, passing the El Cerrito Plaza and El Cerrito del Norte BART stations. From recently planted willows to mature oaks, trees line much of the greenway, enhancing the natural setting and reminding you of the diversity of Northern California's flora.

At the trail's end you reach San Pablo Avenue at Baxter Creek Gateway Park in El Cerrito. The park, a restored urban riparian area, features an amazing diversity of plants and animals in a modestly sized area, including red flowering currant, willows, alder trees, bigleaf maples and Pacific tree frogs. With an assortment of benches, it's a nice place to relax before heading back on the Ohlone Greenway.

DIRECTIONS

To reach the trailhead by car, from San Francisco, take the Bay Bridge to Interstate 80 East. From I-80 take the University Avenue exit toward Berkeley. Continue on University for 2 miles. Turn left on Martin Luther King, Jr., Way. Continue 2 blocks to Hearst Avenue. The trailhead is located at the entrance to Ohlone Park on the northwest corner of Martin Luther King, Jr., Way and Hearst Street. Park on the street.

If you prefer to use public transportation, the Ohlone Greenway can be accessed from the North Berkeley, El Cerrito Plaza, and El Cerrito del Norte BART stations, but be careful to learn about BART regulations if you're bringing your bike.

Contact: City of El Cerrito
Department of Public Works
10890 San Pablo Avenue
El Cerrito, CA 94530
(510) 215-4339
www.el-cerrito.org

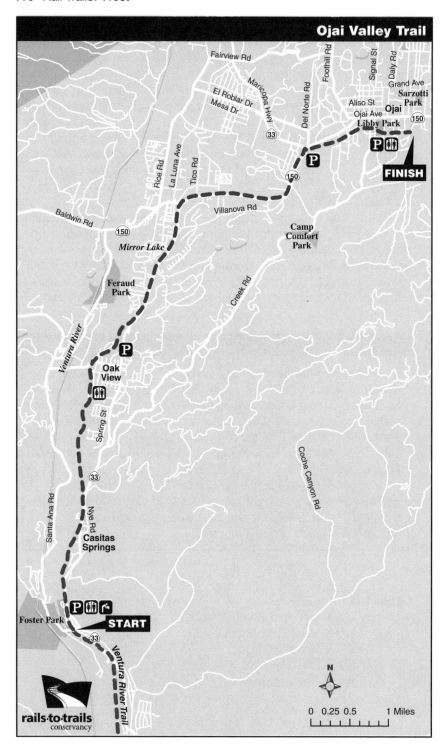

Ojai Valley Trail

Fairview Rd

El Roblar Dr
Mesa Dr

Maricopa Hwy

Del Norte Rd

Foothill Rd

Signal St

Daly Rd

Grand Ave

Sarzotti Park

Aliso St

Ojai Ave **Ojai**

Libby Park

(150)

(33)

Rios Rd

La Luna Ave

Tico Rd

Villanova Rd

Camp Comfort Park

Baldwin Rd

(150)

Mirror Lake

Feraud Park

Creek Rd

Ventura River

Oak View

Spring St

Coche Canyon Rd

(33)

Santa Ana Rd

Nye Rd

Casitas Springs

Foster Park

START

(33)

Ventura River Trail

N

0   0.25 0.5   1 Miles

rails·to·trails
conservancy

FINISH

Ojai Valley Trail

A favorite among rail-trail enthusiasts, the Ojai Valley Trail extends about 9.5 miles north of Ventura from Foster Park in Oak View to the southwestern outskirts of Ojai. Combining this trail with the Ventura River Trail, which extends southward from Foster Park, makes for a memorable, lengthy rail-trail experience.

The smallest city in Ventura County, Ojai is located in the scenic Ojai Valley, surrounded by the peaks of Los Padres National Forest. The city has long been known as a haven for artists, musicians and outdoor enthusiasts. The Chumash Indians were the first known residents of Ojai, and the town's name derives from their word for moon, "A'hwai."

The Ojai Valley Trail follows the former Ventura and Ojai Valley rail line and runs along the Ventura River into the valley. This is a gorgeous ride, providing sweeping views of the surrounding mountains. This trail is

Location
Ventura County

Endpoints
Oak View to Ojai

Mileage
9.5

Roughness Index
1

Surface
Asphalt, woodchips

Packed into the Ojai Valley Trail's gorgeous 9.5 miles are undulating landscapes, horse trails, river crossings and mountainside panoramas.

more rural than the Ventura River Trail to the south, especially where it moves away from Highway 33. There is a gradual uphill grade as you make your way north from the Foster Park trailhead.

The trail is paved and in generally good condition, with a parallel woodchip path for equestrians. Near the 2-mile mark, you pass through an oak grove and then cross a low-lying cement-and-railroad-tie bridge that spans a creek at its confluence with the Ventura River. The trail section close to the bridge is sandy and may be underwater during heavy winter rains. Continuing north, the trail crosses several driveway entrances and roads. Between Loma and Hermosa roads, near mile 7, a sturdy shade structure framed by two large oak trees is equipped with a bench and recycling bins.

At the 8-mile mark, the trail crosses the major intersection of Highways 33 and 150. Cross carefully here and pick up the trail on the other side of Highway 150. At mile 9, you pass through grassy Libby Park, which offers parking, restrooms and access to a trail leading to downtown Ojai. You might want to time your visit to coincide with the Ojai Music Festival, which takes places at the Libby Park Bowl amphitheater in early June. Libby Park also hosts a number of free summer concerts.

DIRECTIONS

To reach the Foster Park trailhead, from downtown Ventura, take Highway 33 heading north. Exit Highway 33 at Casitas Vista Road. Turn right on North Ventura Avenue, and then right again on Casitas Vista Road. The entrance to Foster Park is on the north side of Casitas Vista Road. Parking is available here.

Contact: Public Works Department
City of Ojai
401 South Ventura Street
Ojai, CA 93024
(805) 640-2560
www.ci.ojai.ca.us

Old Railroad Grade

A s it winds up to the eastern peak of Mount Tamalpais in Marin County, this picturesque trail offers an exhilarating combination of far-reaching views, history and challenge. The trail follows the route originally carved out for the Mt. Tamalpais Scenic Railway, which opened in 1896 and soon gained international fame as the "Crookedest Railroad in the World." Boasting a total of 281 curves and 22 trestles, the route featured a unique feat of engineering called the Double Bowknot, a place where a track paralleled itself five times to gain elevation in a very small area on the mountain. Visitors flocked to the railroad, many to experience the "gravity cars," small four-wheel carts that whisked passengers down the mountain at 10 to 12 miles per hour.

Switchbacking up Mount Tamalpais, the Old Railroad Grade is one of California's several former recreational rail corridors that make for a nontraditional but thrilling rail-trail experience.

Like the scenic railway that preceded it, the Old Railroad Grade is anything but typical. It is a steady climb to the 2,571-foot high East Peak (the highest point on Mt. Tam), and you should expect a challenging, and rewarding, trip to the top.

The trail begins at the end of Fern Canyon Road, with ample street parking near the trailhead. If you are feeling particularly ambitious, you can begin in downtown Mill Valley, where the train once started, and ride up to this point. Soon, you come to a fork; bear right and follow signs for the Old Railroad Grade from there.

At 2.5 miles, you arrive at the West Point Inn, the only surviving structure of the railway. A fine spot to take a break and reenergize, the inn offers world-class

Location
Marin County

Endpoints
Fern Canyon Road to East Peak parking lot on Mount Tamalpais

Mileage
4.4

Roughness Index
2

Surface
Ballast, dirt

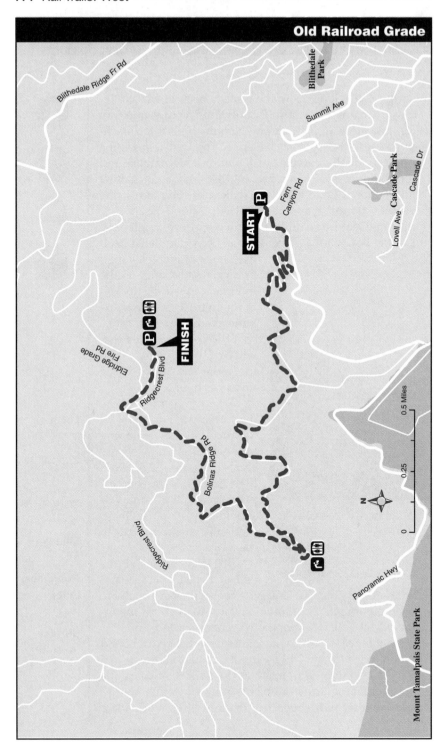

Old Railroad Grade

views that include parts of the East Bay and San Francisco, the Marin Headlands, the Golden Gate Bridge and the Pacific Ocean. The inn hosts regular pancake breakfasts; check its calendar online (www. westpointinn.com) before coming.

You continue to wind up the mountain until you arrive at the East Peak Visitor Center, the end of the trail. From here, you can see parts of nine counties on clear days, including the majestic Sierra Nevada. In addition to the visitor center, there is a snack bar, restrooms, parking lot (you can also drive to the East Peak) and access to a number of hiking trails, including a 0.3-mile plank walk to the lookout tower at the top of the peak. The Mt. Tamalpais Interpretive Association leads a number of hikes from here; check their website (www.mttam.net) if you'd like to coordinate a separate hike with your trip up the Old Railroad Grade.

DIRECTIONS

From San Francisco, take Highway 101 North across the Golden Gate Bridge. Continue on Highway 101 to the Highway 131/Tiburon Boulevard/East Blithedale exit toward East Blithedale Avenue. Continue on East Blithedale Avenue for about 2 miles. Turn left at Throckmorton Avenue, and soon after that turn left on Lovell Avenue. Turn right to stay on Lovell Avenue, then turn right again onto Summit Avenue. Make a sharp left onto Tamalpais Avenue and continue on Tamalpais. Make a slight right onto Summit Avenue and continue on Summit. Turn left on Fern Canyon Road. The trailhead is at the end of Fern Canyon Road; look for the gate. Park on the street.

Contact: Marin Municipal Water District
220 Nellen Avenue
Corte Madera, CA 94925
(415) 945-1586
www.marinwater.org/controller?
action=menuclick&id=242

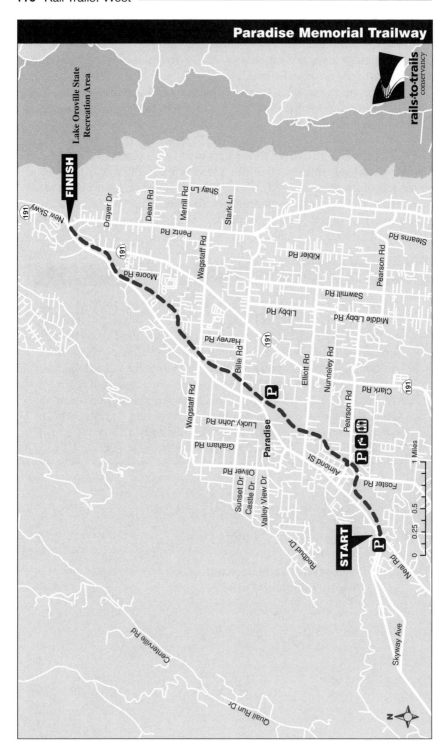

Paradise Memorial Trailway

Paradise Memorial Trailway

L ocated in the Sierra Nevada foothills, Paradise, Calif., is a warm and inviting city with a small-town feel, and this trail offers visitors the perfect way to see it. You can start at either end; the course described here starts on the south end at Neal Road and Skyway Avenue and climbs slightly uphill at an average grade of about 3 percent. If you plan to ride the trail both ways, go south to north so you're riding downhill on the way back.

As you step onto the rail-trail you are surrounded by tall oak woodlands and pine trees. You can soon see houses on your right, but there are so many trees between the trail and the homes that the trail doesn't have a residential feel at all. Likewise, although the trail parallels Skyway Avenue (the city's main road) for most of its route, the abundance of trees between it and the road almost makes you forget this.

The Paradise Memorial Trailway sports a namesake piece of history—the restored Paradise Depot that opened in 1904 and now serves as a museum.

Location
Butte County

Endpoints
Neal Road and Skyway Avenue to 10th Street and Skyway Avenue

Mileage
5.2

Roughness Index
1

Surface
Asphalt

After about a mile the trail turns right onto Black Olive Road. Follow this path into the lovely and well-maintained community park. The park contains restrooms, a playground and the Paradise Depot Museum. The depot opened in 1904 as one of four stations on the Butte County Railroad (BCRR) line, which hauled logs and lumber for the Diamond Match Company operations in Stirling City and Chico. When BCRR added passenger and cargo services, Paradise became the busiest depot on the route. It formed the heart of a new downtown and was a driving force of economic development for the town. Operated by Southern Pacific after 1912, the rail line closed in 1974. Signposts in the park, which occupies the old depot grounds, provide additional information about the history of the railroad and the city of Paradise.

On the other side of the park the path becomes tree-lined again, and remains this way until the end. Less than a mile beyond the park you catch a glimpse of a school to your right through the trees, followed by more houses. If you want to grab a bite to eat or explore the city, you can turn onto Skyway Avenue from one of the crossings along the trail and visit one of several restaurants and delis. The intersection of Skyway Avenue and 10th Street is the endpoint. When you're ready, turn around and get ready for an easy coast back.

DIRECTIONS

To reach the southern trailhead, from Highway 99, take the Paradise exit. Merge onto East Park Avenue, which becomes Skyway Avenue. Continue on Skyway through the town of Paradise to the intersection of Skyway and Neal Road. The trailhead is next to a short brick wall at the intersection that reads TOWN OF PARADISE—WELCOME. There are several nearby shopping centers with ample parking.

To reach the northern trailhead, from Skyway Avenue and Neal Road, continue driving north on Skyway Avenue until you reach the intersection of Skyway and 10th Street. There is no parking lot here, but you can turn right on 10th Street and park on one of the neighborhood streets.

Contact: Paradise Public Works Department
5555 Skyway
Paradise, CA 95969
(530) 872-6291
www.townofparadise.com

Rose Canyon Bicycle Path

This short and sweet trail is a popular route because of its scenery and the important off-street connection it provides between the Mission Bay and University of California at San Diego areas. Tucked between an active rail line and Interstate 5, it offers pleasant views of Rose Canyon's coastal sage- and chaparral-covered hills, and a car-free space to exercise and unwind.

A variety of plants and trees line the corridor, ranging from cattails and native grasses to eucalyptus, madrone and coastal live oak trees. The trail passes through a creek watershed near the 1-mile mark, where you are likely to see ducks and other waterfowl.

Trains are common along this rail-with-trail corridor, so you might see Amtrak's Pacific Surfliner passenger train on its 350-mile route serving communities on the Southern California coast between San Diego and San Luis Obispo.

The Rose Canyon Bicycle Path completes the train-and-traffic landscape of this useful trail tucked between an Amtrak line and Interstate 5.

Location
San Diego County

Endpoints
North end of Santa Fe Street to Gilman and La Jolla Colony drives

Mileage
1.1

Roughness Index
1

Surface
Asphalt

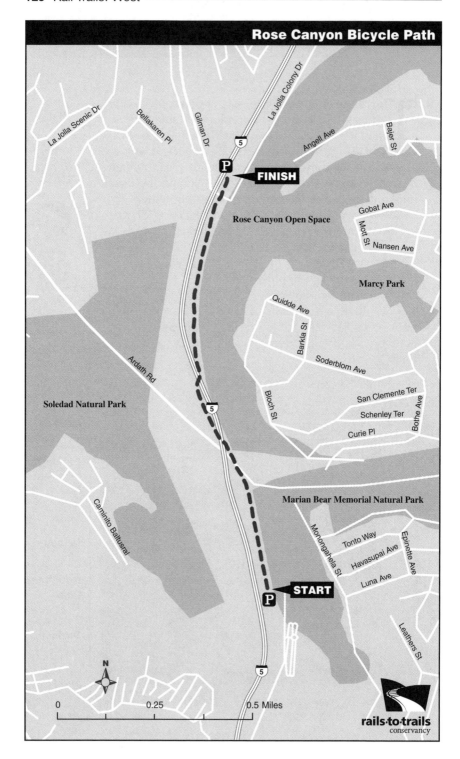

Rose Canyon Bicycle Path

La Jolla Colony Dr

La Jolla Scenic Dr

Bellakaren Pl

Gilman Dr

Angell Ave

Bajer St

P

FINISH

Rose Canyon Open Space

Gobat Ave

Mott St

Nansen Ave

Marcy Park

Quidde Ave

Barkla St

Soderblom Ave

Ardath Rd

Bloch St

San Clemente Ter

Schenley Ter

Bothe Ave

Soledad Natural Park

Curie Pl

Marian Bear Memorial Natural Park

Caminito Battustal

Monongahela St

Tonto Way

Epinette Ave

Havasupai Ave

Luna Ave

P **START**

Leathers St

N

0   0.25   0.5 Miles

rails·to·trails
conservancy

As you near the trail's end, you climb steeply off the grade and up to the trail's intersection with Gilman and La Jolla Colony drives. You can turn around here, continue right (east) onto the bike lane on La Jolla Colony Drive, or bear left (west) and continue on Gilman Drive. Both on-street routes are popular with cyclists and provide connections to longer rides.

The trail's smooth surface is ideal for a variety of activities, including in-line skating and pushing a baby stroller. There are no amenities or restrooms on or near the trail.

If you're interested in becoming more familiar with Rose Canyon, Friends of Rose Canyon hosts regular nature walks. Call (858) 597-0220 or visit www.rosecanyon.org for more information.

DIRECTIONS

To reach the southern endpoint on Santa Fe Street from northbound Interstate 5 in San Diego, take the Balboa/Garnet avenues exit. Head left (west) on Garnet Avenue to Mission Bay Drive and turn right (north). Follow Mission Bay Drive to Damon Avenue and turn right (east) on Damon. Follow Damon Avenue for 0.3 mile to Santa Fe Street and turn left (north). Follow Santa Fe Street north to its end in a cul-de-sac, which has ample parking.

To reach the Santa Fe (southern) endpoint from southbound Interstate 5, take the Balboa/Garnet avenues exit. This puts you on Mission Bay Drive. Turn left (east) onto Damon Avenue, then follow the directions above to reach the trailhead.

To reach the northern endpoint from either northbound or southbound Interstate 5, take the La Jolla colony exit. Go west on Gilman Drive for 0.1 mile to a left-hand turn into the park-and-ride lot, which is on the left (south) side of Gilman Drive. Park here and ride down to the trailhead.

Contact: City of San Diego
1010 Second Avenue, Suite 800
San Diego, CA 92101
(619) 533-3126

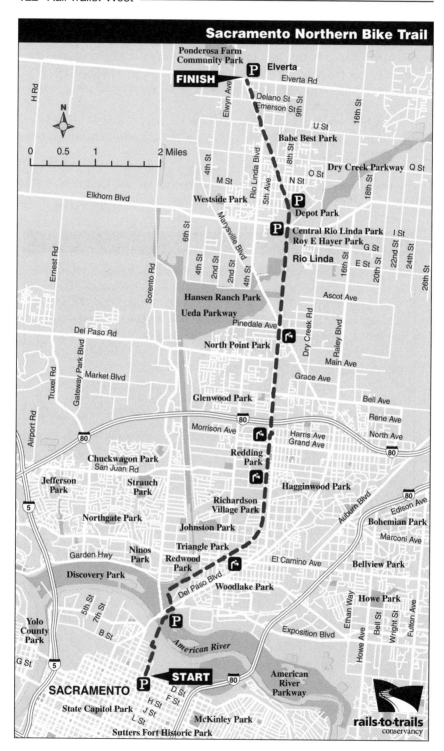

Sacramento Northern Bike Trail

Follow this trail for a tour of Sacramento and its surrounding communities, weaving through historic neighborhoods and parks and finishing in a scenic rural area. The bikeway also connects with a number of other local and regional trails, and serves as a vital community resource for recreation and commuting to work and school.

The trail runs along the former right-of-way of the Sacramento Northern Interurban Railway, which carried passengers between Sacramento and Chico until the line closed in the mid-1940s. Today you can enjoy many of the bridges and structures that were built for the railway.

Begin near downtown Sacramento on C Street between 19th and 20th streets, and head north through an industrial area. After about 0.5 mile, you come to a T junction in the trail, bear right and soon cross a trestle bridge over the American River. At the 1-mile mark, you reach another T junction. Turn left to merge onto the Jedediah

A spin on the Sacramento Northern Bike Trail can double as a city-tour and trail connector.

Location
Sacramento County

Endpoints
Sacramento to Elverta

Mileage
10

Roughness Index
1

Surface
Asphalt

A trestle bridge crosses the American River on the Sacramento Northern Bike Trail.

Smith National Trail. Immediately after crossing Del Paso Boulevard, you enter Discovery Park, a popular spot for recreation boaters and anglers. Bear right at the first fork, and a small rise carries you onto the raised former rail bed, which offers a nice view of the park and its ponds and waterfowl. Another 0.2 mile down the trail you cross an active rail line; from this point on the trail is straight, smooth, flat, tree-lined and landscaped. You'll pass through an attractive metal archway each time you reach a new neighborhood.

Near the 6-mile mark, the trail heads into an agricultural landscape. You cross a series of bridges and ride under canopies of mature trees, with cattle grazing in pastures on both sides of the trail.

Near the 8-mile mark, the trail reaches the Rio Linda Chamber of Commerce and Rio Linda Community Center, which has an adjacent playing field and BMX bike park. The trail continues on a newly constructed segment for another 2 miles, and ends at Elverta Road. You can either ride back to the beginning, or arrange for a shuttle.

There are numerous shaded areas and rest kiosks along the trail where you might want to take a breather, especially if you're visiting during Sacramento's hot summer.

DIRECTIONS

To reach the Sacramento endpoint, from Interstate 80 take the 15th Street (Highway 160) exit. (If you are headed eastbound, take the 16th Street exit.) Go north on 16th Street, which is a one-way road, to D Street. Go right (east) on D Street to 20th street, and turn left (north) on 20th Street to reach C Street. The trail is located between 19th and 20th Streets, on the north side of the road. Ample street parking is available, and a large gateway identifies the trailhead.

To reach the Rio Linda endpoint, from Interstate 5 in Sacramento, head north on I-5 to its junction with Highway 99. Go right (north) on Highway 99 to the Elkhorn Boulevard exit. Follow Elkhorn Boulevard east to Rio Linda Boulevard. Turn left (north) on Rio Linda Boulevard and follow it to Elverta Road. There is a parking lot at the trailhead on Elverta Road.

Contact: Department of Transportation
City of Sacramento
915 I Street, 2nd Floor
Sacramento, CA 95814
(916) 808-8434
www.cityofsacramento.org/transportation

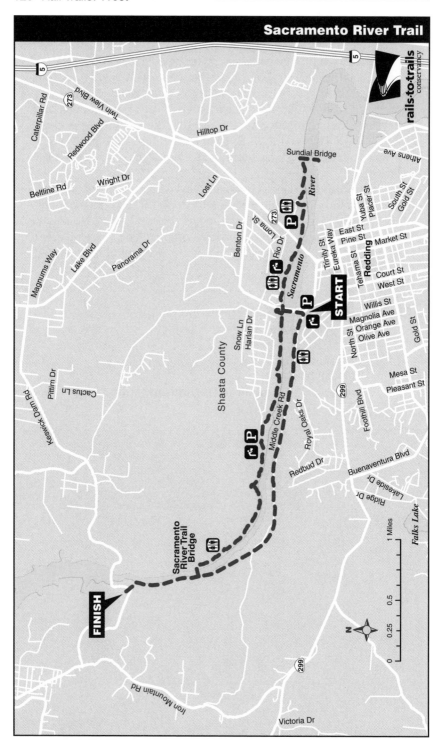

Sacramento River Trail

rails-to-trails
conservancy

Sacramento River Trail

Tucked away in Northern California's Shasta County is the charming town of Redding, which over the years has worked diligently to become one of the premier trail destinations in the West. The pride of Redding's trail system is the Sacramento River Trail, a 10-mile corridor that runs along the banks of the Sacramento River, offering stunning views of the river and nearby mountains, and a close-up look at one of the most breathtaking bicycle/pedestrian bridges in the country. The Sacramento River Trail holds court as a favorite for many California rail-trail enthusiasts.

From the eastern trailhead on Middle Creek you head west along the Sacramento River. A wooded section quickly gives way to an open area with striking views of the Trinity Alps. During the spring months, the river maintains a glacial, deep blue hue from melted snow flowing down from the mountains. The river-powered mining operations during the late 1800s, and

No matter which side of the river you choose to ride, the Sacramento River Trail offers splendid mountain and water vistas.

Location
Shasta County

Endpoints
Middle Creek Road at North Court Street to Sundial Bridge in Redding

Mileage
10

Roughness Index
1

Surface
Asphalt

The Sundial Bridge at the eastern end of the trail, with its glass decking and time-telling functionality writ large, provides a rather spectacular crossing of the Sacramento River.

interpretive signs along the trail explain the hydraulic mining operations. You'll also see remnants of the railroad operated by the Central Pacific Railroad that once carried ore as far north as Portland, Ore.

At the 3-mile mark you come to the Sacramento River Trail Bridge, an impressive 418-foot stress ribbon bridge. Opened in 1990, it was the first bridge of its kind built in North America. The bridge is supported by 236 steel cables inside the bridge deck that are drilled into bedrock. The design allows the bridge to have a minimal impact on the natural rock lining the Sacramento River, and avoids the need for piers.

You can cross the bridge and head east on the other side of the river, or continue another 0.5 mile to the Keswick Dam western trailhead and return.

While the southernmost 3-mile section of the trail has a gradual grade, the northern portion—which is not a rail-trail—is more undulating, with short climbs and dips. The trail meanders through an upscale neighborhood here, and has a variety of local access points. It has a very smooth surface most of the way and gets plenty of use by walkers, runners and cyclists. Near the 6-mile mark, you come to the historic Diestelhorst Bridge. Completed in 1915 and now used exclusively by bicyclists and pedestrians, it was originally the first bridge across the Sacramento River built for automobiles. You can return to the original trailhead by crossing this bridge, or you continue east along the river, where several visual treats await.

One is the lovely McConnell Arboretum, an impressive garden complex surrounded by 200 acres of riparian forest and oak savannah. It features butterfly, children's, medicinal and Pacific Rim gardens, among others. Next to the arboretum is a masterpiece of functional art and the highlight of this trail—the Sundial Bridge. Designed by world-renowned architect Santiago Calatrava and completed in 2004, the bridge is surfaced with translucent structural glass that is illuminated from beneath and glows at night. The bicycle/pedestrian bridge is also a functional sundial, the largest in the world. On the other side of the bridge is the Turtle Bay Aquarium.

Return the way you came. You can either cross the river at the Diestelhorst Bridge or follow the entire route and cross the river farther west at the Sacramento River Trail Bridge and head back along the southern side of the river.

DIRECTIONS

To reach the eastern trailhead, from Interstate 5 in Redding, take the exit for Highways 299 and 44. Head left (west) on Highway 299 toward Eureka. The highway leads into downtown Redding. Signs mark the route of Highway 299 as it winds through town, first heading west on Shasta Street, then right (north) on Pine Street, then left (west) on Eureka Way. Stay on Highway 299. At Eureka Way, follow Eureka Way/Highway 299 to Court Street. Turn right (north) on Court Street and go for a half mile to the parking lot on Middle Creek Road. The lot is on the left (west) side of Court Street just before it crosses a bridge over the Sacramento River.

Contact: Office of Community Services
City of Redding
City Hall, 2nd Floor
777 Cypress Avenue
Redding, CA 96001
(530) 225-4009
www.ci.redding.ca.us

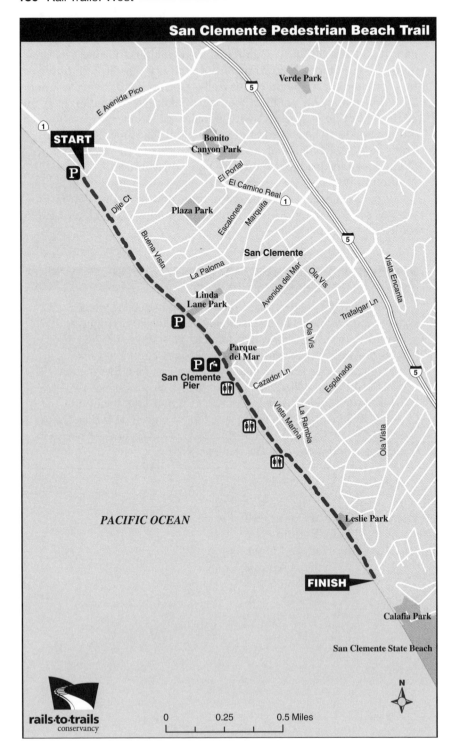

San Clemente Pedestrian Beach Trail

Verde Park

E Avenida Pico

START

Bonito Canyon Park

El Portal

El Camino Real

Plaza Park

Escalones

Marquita

San Clemente

Dije Ct

Buena Vista

La Paloma

Avenida del Mar

Ola Vis

Linda Lane Park

Vista Encanta

Trafalgar Ln

Parque del Mar

Ola Vis

San Clemente Pier

Cazador Ln

Esplanade

Vista Marina

La Rambla

Ola Vista

PACIFIC OCEAN

Leslie Park

FINISH

Calafia Park

San Clemente State Beach

rails·to·trails
conservancy

0   0.25   0.5 Miles

N

San Clemente Pedestrian Beach Trail

Hugging one of the most picturesque shorelines in Southern California, the San Clemente Beach Trail is one of the premier rail-trails in the area. The trail itself is technically a rail-with-trail, as it shares the corridor with an active Amtrak line with service between Los Angeles and San Diego, as well as Metrolink trains that are part of the L.A. commuter rail system.

Whereas most communities surrounding L.A. have fallen victim to rampant development, surfside San Clemente has preserved its small town identity and spirit. The trail enhances these qualities. The trail surface is composed mostly of compact sand from the beach.

Begin at the north end of the pedestrian-only trail near the San Clemente Metrolink station in the area known as North Beach. The trail leads south out of the Metrolink parking lot. It is narrowly situated between high cliffs on the left and the railroad tracks and beach on the right. Be sure to check out the unique flora that

The San Clemente Pedestrian Beach Trail shares its corridor with Amtrak and Metrolink trains, making it one of the most picturesque, scenic rail-with-trails in the country.

Location
Orange County

Endpoints
San Clemente/
North Beach
Metrolink Station to
San Clemente State
Beach

Mileage
2.3

Roughness Index
2

Surface
Compact sand
and pavement

covers the cliff, as well as the impressive beach houses high atop the cliffs.

After several hundred yards, the trail flows onto an impressive bridge. Running about 10 feet off the ground for roughly a quarter mile, the bridge serves as a glorified boardwalk over sensitive beach habitat.

Once across the bridge, follow the trail across the railroad tracks and continue to the primary beachfront area of San Clemente at the Pier Bowl trailhead. Here you will find a plethora of restaurants, shops and beach picnic areas. A pier juts out into the ocean here, and is a prime location for watching surfers ride the waves. There are public restrooms and plenty of parking near the pier.

The trail continues south along the beach and crosses the railroad tracks again about a quarter mile beyond the Pier Bowl area. Be careful because the crossing is at grade with the tracks. The trail continues for another 1.5 miles south along the beach to the endpoint near San Clemente State Beach, which has parking and beach access.

DIRECTIONS

To reach the northern trailhead at the Metrolink station, from Interstate 5, take Exit 76 and head west on East Avenida Pico. Follow it for about 0.5 mile to the intersection of North El Camino Real. Take a right and the train station will be on your left in a few hundred feet.

To reach the trailhead at the Pier Bowl area, from Interstate 5 take the exit and head (right or left) west into town. Take a left onto North El Camino Real Road. Continue for less than 0.5 mile to Avenida del Mar. Take a left and follow Avenida del Mar all the way to the beach and San Clemente Pier, and the adjoining parking lots. The trailhead is just beyond the train tracks.

Contact: San Clemente State Beach
California State Parks
Department of Parks and Recreation
1416 9th Street
Sacramento, CA 95814
(949) 492-3156
www.parks.ca.gov/?page_id=646

Shepherd Canyon Trail

Tucked in the quiet Oakland hills neighborhood of Montclair, the Shepherd Canyon Trail is a popular community rail-trail that has come to symbolize the power of community activism. The rail right-of-way, which was once used by Sacramento Northern Railroad as part of a regional interurban electric rail system, was at risk of becoming Highway 77 during the 1970s. Community activists and visionary local officials prevented the highway from being constructed through Shepherd Canyon and instead created the trail to preserve open space and encourage alternative modes of transportation.

Climb the canyon on the namesake Shepherd Canyon Trail that winds through the Oakland hills and links charming neighbors and neighborhoods alike.

The trail begins in quaint Monclair Village, near an assortment of cafes, shops and restaurants that you may want to visit before or after your time on the trail. Minutes after entering the trail, you are enveloped in a canopy of oak and eucalyptus trees, distanced from the hustle and bustle of the village. Shepherd Canyon is a popular neighborhood trail, with a healthy mix of dog walkers, parents pushing strollers, cyclists, joggers and folks just out for a stroll. Many segments of the trail are lined with houses, and it's apparent that the trail has been adopted as a community amenity and treasure. There are also a number of unpaved side trails for further exploration.

Farther along the trail, the Snake Road overpass bridge is where a Sacramento Northern trestle once stood. Immediately after crossing the bridge, an open area with benches and a nice vista of the Oakland hills

Location
Alameda County

Endpoints
Medau Place at Mountain Boulevard to Saroni Drive at Shepherd Canyon Drive

Mileage
1.4

Roughness Index
1

Surface
Asphalt, crushed stone

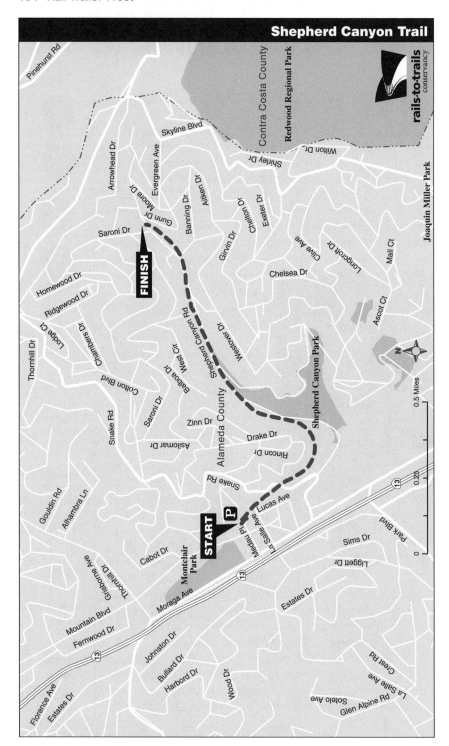

Shepherd Canyon Trail

makes for an ideal spot to take in the ambience and watch trail users go by.

The trail gradually climbs up the canyon, with a steeper section for the last half mile. The trail ends at the intersection of Saroni Drive and Shepherd Canyon Drive. Cyclists looking for a longer ride can continue on Shepherd Canyon Drive and connect with Skyline Boulevard, a popular on-road cycling route.

DIRECTIONS

From San Francisco or downtown Oakland, take Interstate 980 East toward Walnut Creek/Highway 24 East. Exit onto Highway 24 East and continue for about 4 miles. Take the exit for Highway 13 South toward Hayward. From Highway 13, take the Moraga Avenue exit toward Thornhill Drive. Keep left at the fork, follow signs for Montclair District/Moraga Avenue East/Thornhill Drive and merge onto Moraga Avenue. Moraga Avenue merges onto Mountain Boulevard. Turn left at Medau Place and go 2 blocks until the street dead-ends at the trailhead. You can park on the street or in the nearby lot.

Contact: Office of Parks and Recreation
City of Oakland
250 Frank Ogawa Plaza, Suite 3330
Oakland, CA 94612
(510) 238-7275
www.oaklandnet.com/Parks

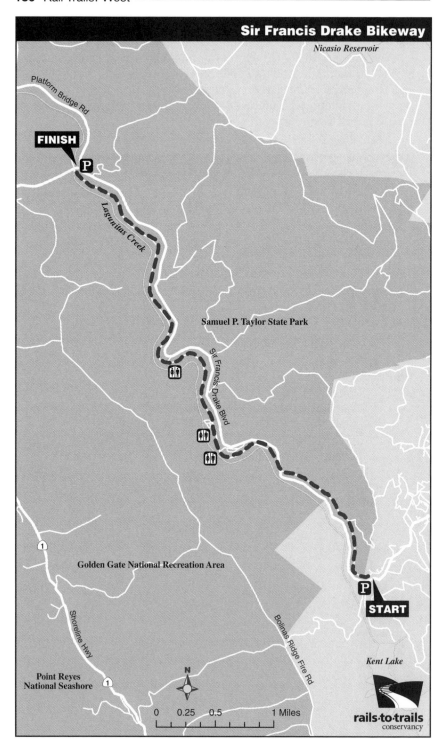

Sir Francis Drake Bikeway

Nicasio Reservoir

Platform Bridge Rd

FINISH

P

Lagunitas Creek

Samuel P. Taylor State Park

Sir Francis Drake Blvd

1

Golden Gate National Recreation Area

Shoreline Hwy

Bolinas Ridge Fire Rd

P

START

Kent Lake

Point Reyes National Seashore

1

N

0   0.25   0.5   1 Miles

rails·to·trails
conservancy

Sir Francis Drake Bikeway

The spectacular Sir Francis Drake Bikeway (also known as the Cross Marin Trail) sits on the re-cycled roadbed of the former North Pacific Coast Railroad, which used to run from Larkspur to Cazadero. This family-friendly rail-trail provides a safe and enjoyable way for visitors to access the swimming holes in Lagunitas Creek and the redwood groves that have made the park so popular.

Unpaved at the southern trailhead, the path begins in fairly dense woods. On your left are thick redwood stands cushioned by undergrowth of sorrel, and an abundance of ferns. On your right is the lovely Lagunitas Creek. At mile 1.5, you arrive at a wooden bridge with a red SALMON CROSSING sign. Silver salmon and steelhead trout migrate up Lagunitas Creek to spawn during the winter, and this is the first of several spots along the trail where you can view them. If you are lucky, you may also catch a glimpse of the beavers that sometimes work in the area.

Woodsy but not too wild, the Sir Francis Drake Bikeway winds through impressive redwood groves.

At about mile 2 the road becomes paved and you reach Samuel P. Taylor State Park. Samuel Taylor, an entrepreneur from Boston, struck it rich during the California gold rush. He used a portion of his wealth to create a resort and recreational campground called Camp Taylor, which was one of the first sites in the U.S. to offer camping as a recreational activity. In the 1870s and 1880s, it was quite popular for families to take the railroad out to Camp Taylor for the weekend.

Location
Marin County

Endpoints-
Shafter's Bridge
to Platform Bridge
Road

Mileage
5.3

**Roughness
Index**
2

Surface
Asphalt, dirt

Continuing on, you pass the Redwood Grove Group Picnic area on the right and another campsite a quarter mile farther. When the weather is nice, the campgrounds are usually full, though the campers and facilities do not detract from the natural beauty of this wooded area. Oak, tanoak, madrone, live oak, laurel and Douglas fir are all visible along the path. The path is also lined with California native buttercups, Indian paintbrush and milkmaids. Black-tailed deer is the most common animal in the park and can often be spotted from the trail.

You pass another restroom at mile 3. The last 2.3 miles of the trail is paved and shaded by the cool redwood groves it parallels. You can extend your trail day if you aren't ready to turn around at the endpoint, as there are numerous trail networks in the vicinity.

DIRECTIONS

To reach the southern trailhead, from Highway 101, exit on Sir Francis Drake Boulevard. Head west on Sir Francis Drake Boulevard toward San Anselmo for about 18 miles. At the intersection of Sir Francis Drake Boulevard and Platform Bridge Road, turn left. The trailhead is at the end of the short metal bridge on your right. On the left is a small parking lot with a one-hour limit. There are various places to pull off and park along Sir Francis Drake Boulevard without time limits.

To reach the northern trailhead, from Highway 101, exit on Sir Francis Drake Boulevard. Drive past the intersection of Sir Francis Drake Boulevard and Platform Bridge Road, crossing over a concrete bridge. Shortly after crossing the bridge you see an unmarked road on your right. Turn right on this road, then turn left and park on an abandoned concrete street. Walk toward an old bridge. The trail entrance is marked with a large sign that says CROSS MARIN TRAIL.

Contact: Samuel P. Taylor State Park
P.O. Box 251
Lagunitas, CA 94938
(415) 488-9897
www.parks.ca.gov/?page_id=469

Sonoma Bike Path

If you are attracted to the rolling, wine country landscapes and historical architecture of Sonoma Valley, the Sonoma Bike Path won't disappoint. Located in the heart of historic Sonoma, just over an hour from downtown San Francisco, the rail-trail passes scenic vineyards, historic mansions, beautiful parks and an old railroad depot museum.

Park your car at Maxwell Farms Regional Park just off Highway 12. After crossing Verona Avenue and taking a right on Highway 12, you will pick up the trail about a quarter mile down the road on your left. This marked western end of the trail, which is heavily used by local commuters, is tucked tastefully between a residential area and small Olsen Park. After about a half mile, the bike path crosses into Sonoma Historical State Park, which features various sites of cultural and historical significance. As you enter the open expanse of the park with its lush, sandy green lawns, you'll immediately spot on

The Sonoma Bike Path features several historical sites, including a restored railroad depot, boxcars and caboose in Sonoma Historical State Park.

Location
Sonoma County

Endpoints
Maxwell Farms
Regional Park to
4th Street East

Mileage
1.5

**Roughness
Index**
2

Surface
Asphalt

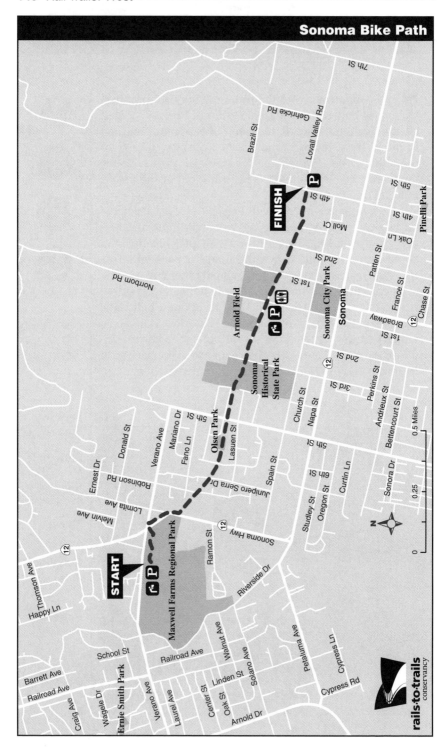

your left the main attraction of the park, the 1840 home of General Mariano Vallejo, La Casa Grande. General Vallejo was appointed as the first Commandante General for California by Mexico, when it gained independence from Spain. La Casa Grande was one of the finest residences in 19th-century California.

After continuing through Sonoma Historical State Park for a half mile, you enter an area known as Depot Park. On your right are old orange boxcars and an orange train caboose in front of the Depot Park Museum. Housed in the old Northwestern Pacific Railroad Depot, the museum contains many historical artifacts about the Sonoma Valley Railroad Company, which used to operate this line, and also contains documents, maps and photographs of Sonoma's rich cultural past—it's definitely worth a visit.

East of the Depot Museum, the trail traverses a lovely section of farmland known as the Patch, where you can enjoy a colorful array of locally grown produce. A half mile past the Depot Museum, the trail ends at 4th Street next to the Sebastiani Vineyards and Winery. If you have time, go past the winery on 4th Street and take the next right on East Spain Street. Continue until you reach the beautiful and historic Sonoma Plaza surrounded by stately Sonoma City Hall and numerous shops and restaurants.

Parking is available at Sebastiani Vineyards and Winery on 4th Street and Lovall Valley Drive, and you could start your ride from this end of the trail as well.

This section of the Sonoma Bike Path is nicknamed the "Patch" for its array of trailside farmland and produce.

DIRECTIONS

To reach the western trailhead at Maxwell Farms Regional Park, head north on Highway 101 toward San Antonio Road. Take the Highway 116 East exit toward Napa/Sonoma and turn left on Highway 116 East/Lakeville Highway. Take a left at Frates Road and continue straight onto Adobe Road. Take another left at Stage Gulch Road and then take a slight left at Arnold Drive. Turn right at West Verano Avenue to enter Maxwell Farms Regional Park. The park charges a $5 parking fee. To access the trailhead from Santa Rosa, take Highway 12 (Sonoma Highway) south for 18 miles and take a right at West Verano Avenue to access the park.

To reach the eastern trailhead at Sebastiani Winery, head north on Highway 101 toward San Antonio Road. Take the Highway 116 East exit toward Napa/Sonoma and turn left on Highway 116 East/ Lakeville Highway. Take a left at Frates Road and continue straight onto Abode Road. Take another left at Stage Gulch Road and then take a slight left at Arnold Drive. Turn left at West Watmaugh Road and turn left again on Broadway. Take a right at East Napa Street and a left on East 4th Street where you'll find the parking lot on the right.

Contact: Sonoma County Bicycle Coalition
P.O. Box 3088
Santa Rosa, CA 95402
(707) 545-0153
http://bikesonoma.org/index.html

Sugar Pine Railway-Strawberry Branch

For more than 50 years in the early 1900s, the Sugar Pine Railway operated steam trains to haul logs along the Stanislaus River for the Standard Lumber Company, and later the Pickering Lumber Company. Today this wooded corridor hosts a gentle 3-percent grade rail-trail that can be enjoyed by hikers, mountain bikers, equestrians and, in the winter months, cross-country skiers. The trail represents a very small part of the Sugar Pine Railway system, which included about 70 miles of main line and almost 400 miles of spurs and branches. While there are a number of rail-trails in the Sierra Nevada due to the area's extensive logging history, this is one of the easiest and most family-friendly because of its easy accessibility, gentle grade and relatively forgiving dirt surface.

Begin at the Fraser Flat Road trailhead for a nicely shaded, gradual uphill grade that affords great views of the majestic South Fork of the Stanislaus River below.

The Sugar Pine Railway-Strawberry Branch generally follows the Stanislaus River and is one of the easiest and smoothest of the logging corridors in the Sierra Nevada.

Location
Tuolumne County

Endpoints
Fraser Flat Road at South Fork of Stanislaus River to Old Strawberry Road

Mileage
5

Roughness Index
3

Surface
Dirt

143

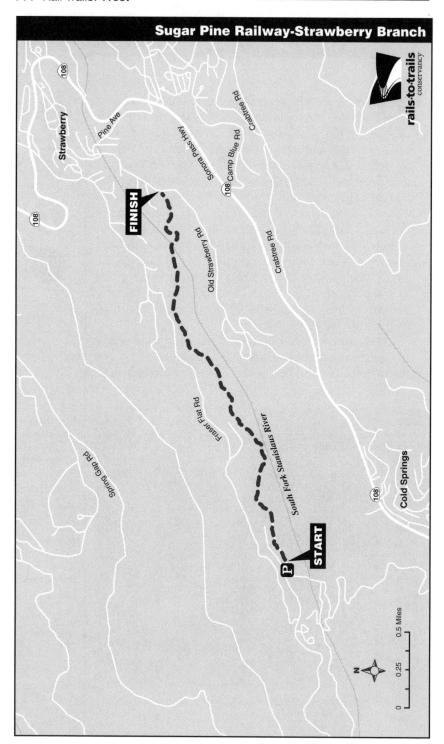

Sugar Pine Railway-Strawberry Branch

rails·to·trails
conservancy

Strawberry

108

Pine Ave

Sonora Pass Hwy

Crabtree Rd

108 Camp Blue Rd

Crabtree Rd

FINISH

108

Old Strawberry Rd

Fraser Flat Rd

Spring Gap Rd

South Fork Stanislaus River

Cold Springs

108

START

P

N

0   0.25   0.5 Miles

The dirt trail surface can be loose in places, and there are some considerable dips in the trail—be careful and keep your eye on what's ahead. At the 1.5-mile mark, halfway through the trail, pass through an unlocked cattle fence and continue. Near the 2.5-mile mark, the trail opens up into a meadow. Here the trail becomes less obvious, but across the meadow you can see where it reenters the forest.

Interpretive tour signs along the trail point out historical highlights. The signs are numbered for use with an informational brochure that you can pick up at the Summit and Mi-Wok Ranger District offices of Stanislaus National Forest. It's a good idea to pick up a map of the area while you're there—the roads aren't well-marked and finding your way around can be challenging.

The trail ends when it intersects Old Strawberry Road at mile 3. For a longer ride, head south (right) on Old Strawberry Road to visit the historic logging town of Strawberry. Your return trip on the trail to Fraser Flat Road is downhill.

DIRECTIONS

To reach the Mi-Wok Ranger District office, head east from Modesto on Highway 108 for about 63 miles. From the district office, turn right (northeast) back onto Highway 108 and continue for about 9 miles to Fraser Flat Road (Forest Road 4N01). Turn left and continue downhill to the bridge at the South Fork of the Stanislaus River. The trailhead (which has no signs) and parking are adjacent to the river, on the south side of the road.

Contact: Mi-Wok Ranger District
Stanislaus National Forest
24695 Highway 108
Mi Wuk Village, CA 95346
(209) 586-0262
www.fs.fed.us/r5/stanislaus/miwok

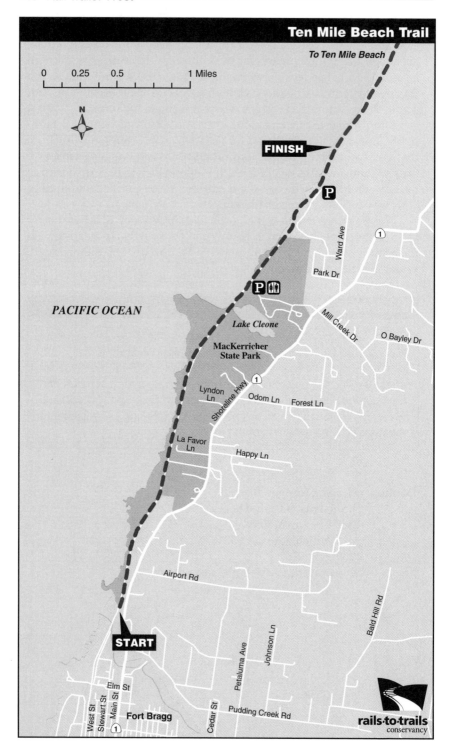

Ten Mile Beach Trail

To Ten Mile Beach

0   0.25   0.5   1 Miles

N

FINISH

P

Ward Ave

① 1

Park Dr

P 🚻

PACIFIC OCEAN

Mill Creek Dr

O Bayley Dr

Lake Cleone

MacKerricher State Park

① 1

Lyndon Ln

Shoreline Hwy

Odom Ln

Forest Ln

La Favor Ln

Happy Ln

Airport Rd

Johnson Ln

Bald Hill Rd

START

Elm St

West St

Stewart St

Main St

Petaluma Ave

Cedar St

① 1

Fort Bragg

Pudding Creek Rd

rails·to·trails
conservancy

Ten Mile Beach Trail

The scenic Ten Mile Beach Trail, also referred to by locals as the MacKerricher Haul Road Trail, is part of an old road used to transport lumber from the Ten Mile River watershed to a mill in Fort Bragg. It begins at the Pudding Creek Trestle near downtown Fort Bragg and ends at Ten Mile River (so named because it is located 10 miles north of the Noyo River). It hugs the Pacific coastline, traveling across a unique and environmentally sensitive sand dune area. Due to the fragile dynamics of the coastal dune environments, the northernmost 5 miles of the trail are no longer accessible by bicycle, but you can still travel the whole trail by foot or on horseback.

From Pudding Creek, you cross a bridge that was the start of the lumber trading route terminating many hundreds of miles away in Eureka 150 years ago. Built in 1915–1916 by the Union Lumber Co., this bridge is the only original railroad trestle remaining on the corridor. Beyond the trestle are 4 miles of coastal bluff. As you move along the trail, you see sweeping vistas of the ocean and a variety of plant and animal species. You might be able to spot the endangered western snowy plover, a bird that typically breeds in dune-backed coastal habitats. Be sure to bring binoculars for whale and seal watching. This stretch is one of the largest uninterrupted whale-watching spots on the western coast. Pacific gray whales can be seen on their migration route from December to April every year.

Pause in your ride on the Ten Mile Beach Trail—this stretch is one of the largest uninterrupted whale-watching spots on the west coast.

Location
Mendocino County

Endpoints
Pudding Creek Trestle to Ten Mile River

Mileage
3.5

Roughness Index
2

Surface
Asphalt, dirt, sand

At about 1.5 miles in, you cross Virgin Creek, a great spot to sit and watch the waves and contemplate a coastline that was 3 to 5 miles farther west around 12,000 years ago. Continuing north you reach sand, the geological terrain that MacKerricher State Park is known for. Dune grasses, some native and some invasive, prevent the dunes from shifting too much. After about another mile you'll see Lake Cleone, a lovely tidal lagoon filled with a variety of birds. There is also a restroom at the lake.

Some sections of the trail near the lake have eroded away and are not bikeable. They are relatively small, however, and can be gone around quite easily by dismounting and walking across the obvious erosions. After the eroded sections, the trail continues north along high bluffs, with breathtaking ocean views. A short distance ahead at approximately 3 miles in is the end of the rideable terrain. Turn around and head back, or park your bike and take a longer coastal walk to Ten Mile River.

DIRECTIONS

To reach the southern trailhead, from Highway 1 in Fort Bragg, head north, passing the old railroad trestle over Pudding Creek. Continue past the first motel north of the trestle and park in the dirt lot north of the Beachcomber Motel at Pudding Creek Beach. You can access the trail from the beach.

To reach the main entrance of MacKerricher State Park, from Highway 1, drive 3 miles north of Fort Bragg and turn left (west) into the park. Follow signs to the Laguna Point Parking area. Day-use parking is free.

There is no parking at Ten Mile River at the north end.

This trail is wheelchair accessible between Pudding Creek and the entrance of MacKerricher State Park.

Contact: MacKerricher State Park
24100 MacKerricher Park Road
Fort Bragg, CA 95437
(707) 964-9112
www.parks.ca.gov/?page_id=436

Tiburon Historical Trail

If you're looking for a gentle rail-trail in Marin County that offers stunning views of both San Francisco Bay and Mt. Tamalpais, the Tiburon Historical Trail is for you. Known alternately as the Tiburon Bike Path and Tiburon Linear Park, the trail begins at Blackie's Pasture, a scenic landing named after a celebrated swaybacked, retired cavalry horse named Blackie that once roamed here.

Soon after beginning the trail you pass the coastal mudflats of Richardson Bay, transition zones between land and sea that host a wide variety of plants and wildlife. A bird—and birder's—paradise, Richardson Bay hosts more than 1 million migratory birds every year, along with a diverse mix of year-round residents, including great blue herons, snowy egrets and red-tailed hawks. Breathtaking views of the bay start here, and they stay with you for the remainder of the trail. Take it all in and enjoy!

The Tiburon Historical Trail offers unfettered views of Richardson Bay where more than 1 million migratory birds flock every year.

Location
Marin County

Endpoints
Tiburon Ferry Terminal to Blackie's Pasture

Mileage
2.6

Roughness Index
1

Surface
Asphalt, ballast

149

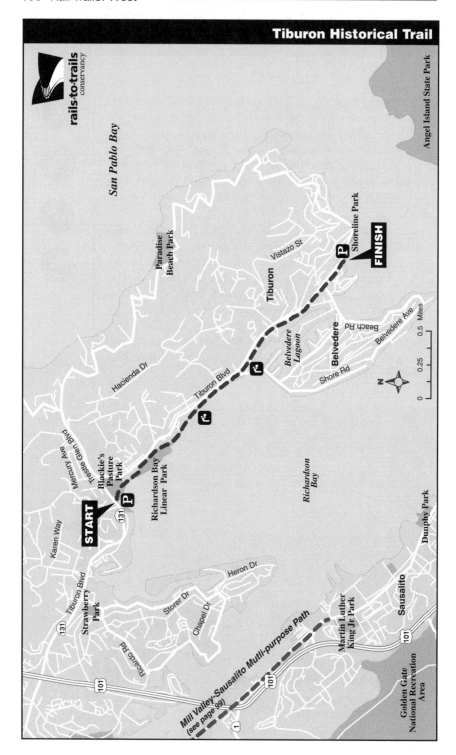

Tiburon Historical Trail

The Tiburon Historical Trail passes a number of playgrounds, small parks and playing fields, so it's very family-friendly and a great destination for a picnic or afternoon outing. It's also very popular with cyclists and joggers, and with a paved section for cyclists and a wide dirt shoulder for walkers and joggers there's ample room for both.

The trail runs along the coast through Tiburon and into Belvedere. Now among the most exclusive communities in the San Francisco Bay Area, both had humble beginnings. In the early 1900s, Tiburon was a blue-collar railroad town, with cargo trains running daily. One of the railroad's "most famous deliveries" was Al Capone, who was carried by train to Alcatraz in 1934. Belvedere, meanwhile, once hosted the ever-pungent McCollam Fish Factory.

At about mile 2, the path becomes an on-street bike lane along Tiburon Boulevard. Continue into downtown Tiburon and the trail's end in Shoreline Park at the ferry terminal. Here you'll find more great views of the bay, a host of restaurants and shops, and the perfect spot to watch the sun set. The terminal is also a great launching point for more adventures: You can take a ferry to nearby Angel Island or San Francisco, or continue along the Paradise Loop, a popular on-street route for cyclists.

DIRECTIONS

To reach the trailhead from San Francisco, take Highway 101 North across the Golden Gate Bridge. Continue on Highway 101, take the Highway 131/Tiburon Boulevard/East Blithedale exit toward Tiburon Boulevard. Continue on Tiburon Boulevard for about 1.5 miles. Look for Blackie's Pasture on the right. The trailhead is at the southern end of the parking lot.

This trail is accessible by ferry from San Francisco. The Blue & Gold Fleet runs a few trips each day between Pier 39 in San Francisco and Tiburon. You can even rent a bicycle in San Francisco and take it on the ferry with you. For more information, visit www.blueandgoldfleet.com/Ferry.

Contact: Department of Public Works
Town of Tiburon
199 Kleinert Way
Tiburon, CA 94920
(415) 435-7388
www.ci.tiburon.ca.us

Truckee River Bike Trail

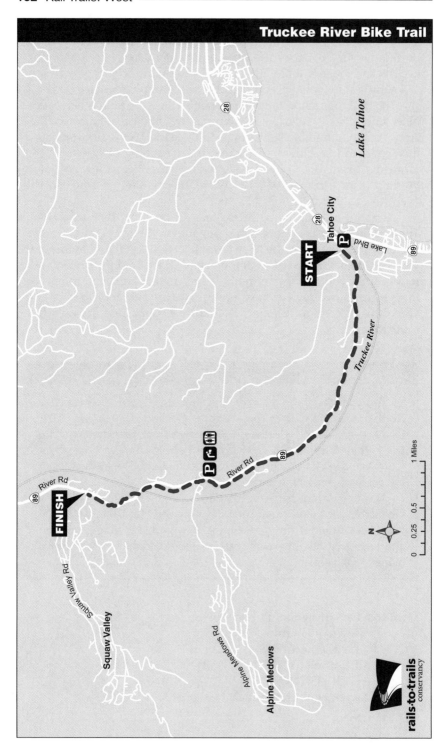

rails-to-trails conservancy

Truckee River Bike Trail

The popular Truckee River Bike Trail is an ideal rail-trail in many ways. Its smooth, flat surface provides all types of users with a scenic easy-to-negotiate route from Tahoe City to Squaw Valley. It connects in both directions to other paths for users who want a longer stroll or ride, and there are facilities for many recreational activities, such as fishing, picnicking and river rafting, along or near the trail. Plus, the Truckee River that it parallels is magnificent.

In the summer both the trail and river are filled with people enjoying the outdoors. The river is slow-moving during this time of year, and floating down it is a popular pastime for folks of all ages. There are several places along the trail where people can stop to fish for trout. In the springtime, the river moves quickly and the rapids swell. There aren't as many tourists here at this time, which gives the rail-trail a calmer, more tranquil feel.

Linked to 165 miles of additional bike trails, the Truckee River Bike Trail is a peaceful rail-trail alternative to some of the more intense mountain biking options in the Tahoe Rim area.

Location
Placer County

Endpoints
Tahoe City to
Midway Bridge in
Squaw Valley

Mileage
4

**Roughness
Index**
1

Surface
Asphalt, dirt

153

Embark on the trail at Tahoe City. For the first few miles, you are treated to dazzling scenery of the river on your left and evergreen trees on your right. At about 3.5 miles in, you climb a short hill and then come to the River Ranch Lodge on your left. An excellent place to stop for a drink or a bite to eat, the lodge overlooks the river and offers fantastic views. Continuing along the trail past the lodge, you cross Alpine Meadows Road before the trail ends at the Midway Bridge. To extend your trip from here, you can detour through Squaw Valley to the base of the ski resort. A 2.3-mile bike path runs the entire length of the valley, paralleling Squaw Valley Road and ending at the Squaw Valley USA ski resort.

Near the start point in Tahoe, the Tahoe Rim Trail (TRT) also connects with the Truckee River Bike Trail. The 165-mile TRT loops around the lake and offers sufficient miles of path for even the sturdiest of cyclists to explore.

DIRECTIONS

The Tahoe City trailhead is located off of Highway 89 and Fairway Drive. From Interstate 80, exit south on State Highway 89 and proceed 12 miles to Tahoe City. About a quarter mile after you enter Tahoe City, you will see Fairway Drive on your left. Turn here and look for parking in one of several nearby lots on your right.

The Midway Bridge trailhead is not an advisable starting point.

Contact: Tahoe City Public Utility District
221 Fairway Drive
Tahoe City, CA 96145
(530) 583-3796
www.tahoecitypud.com

Tulare Santa Fe Trail

The Tulare Santa Fe Trail is located in the heart of the Central San Joaquin Valley, one of the most productive agriculture areas in the world. The trail extends east to west across the central portion of the town of Tulare, connecting residential areas at each end with the downtown commercial area. The Tulare Santa Fe occupies a wide corridor, with newly planted trees and landscaping, separate biking and equestrian components, trail lighting in the central business area, distance markings each mile, and multiple rest stops featuring benches and drinking fountains. The trail runs along a former spur line for the Southern Pacific and Burlington Northern/Santa Fe railroads, which once played a key role in transporting locally grown crops to markets across the country. The rail line ceased operations in 1989, and the trail was completed in 2004.

The Tulare Santa Fe Trail runs through the heart of Tulare, connecting both ends of town, several schools and neighborhoods to the central business area.

The trail can be accessed easily along its entire length. Virtually all of Tulare's schools are within a half mile of the trail, providing a ready corridor for safe student travel. Near mile 1, you'll come to Live Oak Park, the city's large, multiuse park, which lies adjacent to the trail on the northern side. This is also the site where the city's new library is slated to be built. The central portion of the trail passes directly through the downtown and redevelopment area. Enclosed on both sides with white picket fencing, the equestrian trail is particularly attractive. (This trail segment does not extend through the downtown area.)

Location
Tulare County

Endpoints
East Prosperity Avenue to West Inyo Drive and Soults Drive

Mileage
4.5

Roughness Index
1

Surface
Asphalt, dirt

155

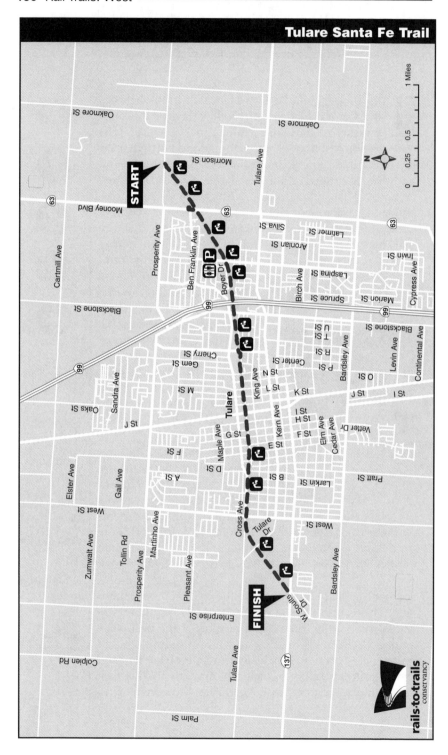

Plans are under way to extend the rail-trail 7 miles north to the larger city of Visalia.

If you're new to the area and have some extra time, you might consider taking the 45-minute trip north from Tulare to Sequoia National Park, which straddles the Sierra Nevada. Sequoia Park is home to a special natural treasure: General Sherman, the biggest tree in the world.

DIRECTIONS

To reach the northeast trailhead, exit Highway 99 at East Prosperity Avenue. Follow the road east for 1.6 miles. The trailhead is on the right. There is no parking here, but a shopping center 0.5 mile west on East Prosperity has plenty of parking.

To reach the southwest trailhead, exit Highway 99 at East Tulare Avenue (Highway 137). Go west for 0.8 mile, turn left and follow M Street for two blocks. Turn right and follow West Inyo Avenue for 2 miles. The trailhead is at the intersection of West Inyo and West Soults Drive. There is no parking at the trailhead, but you can look for parking in the neighborhood south of West Soults Drive. This trail is wheelchair accessible.

Contact: Parks and Library Department
City of Tulare Recreation
830 South Blackstone Street
Tulare, CA 93274
(559) 684-4310
www.ci.tulare.ca.us

Tustin Trail-Esplanade Avenue

rails·to·trails
conservancy

Tustin Trail-Esplanade Avenue

If you are looking for a quick escape from the smog and traffic of Southern California, take a trip along the Tustin Trail-Esplanade Avenue. This short trail winds through quiet, palm-tree filled neighborhoods of Tustin in Orange County. Feel the Santa Ana winds as they blow your worries away on this pleasant trail.

The Tustin Trail-Esplanade Avenue occupies a wide strip of land, providing much more park space than a traditional trail. One reason not to miss this Southern California gem is the landscaping; the colorful flowers and shrubs that line the trail make for a serene experience. The hard-packed clay trail surface is comfortable for all types of trail use. You are likely to meet friendly locals out enjoying the trail.

The Tustin Trail-Esplanade Avenue provides Orange County residents with a brief respite from crowds and concrete.

Beginning at the intersection of Fairhaven and Esplanade avenues, the trail parallels Esplanade Avenue as it heads south. The trail does have two busy road crossings, the first at East 17th Street about a half mile from the start and the second at Vanderlip Avenue, about a quarter mile from the end of the trail.

Just beyond Vanderlip Avenue, the trail runs past, and serves as a wonderful outdoor outlet to urban Guin Foss Elementary School. A short distance beyond the school, the trail ends at Warren Avenue.

Two other short sections of the Tustin Trail located nearby are not covered here. Visit www.traillink.com for more information about them.

Location
Orange County

Endpoints
Fairhaven and
Esplanade avenues
to Warren Avenue

Mileage
1

**Roughness
Index**
1

Surface
Dirt

DIRECTIONS

Though the trail's endpoints are bookended by Warren and Fairhaven avenues, parking is only available at the Vanderlip Avenue trailhead. To reach the Vanderlip Avenue trailhead, from the Santa Ana Freeway, take the Newport Avenue exit and head north for about a mile. Take a left onto Vanderlip Avenue. Follow Vanderlip Avenue for about 0.25 mile. You will see Guin Foss Elementary School and a public parking lot on your left. The trail is adjacent to this lot.

Contact: Orange County Transportation Authority
550 South Main Street
P.O. Box 14184
Orange, CA 92868
(714) 636-RIDE (7433)
www.octa.net

Ventura River Trail

This trail follows the former Ventura and Ojai Valley Railroad right-of-way from Main Street in Ventura north to Foster Park northeast of town. The Ventura River Trail, also known as the Ojai Valley Trail Extension, has a distinctly industrial feel to it, and it gives trail users a close-up look at the many businesses (both past and present) that have fueled the region's growth. Opened in 1999, the trail links the Ojai Valley Trail and Omer Rains Trail for a spectacular 17-mile urban bike ride that extends from historic Ventura Pier to Fox Street in Ojai.

The Ventura River Trail parallels Highway 33 and Ventura Avenue, but the roads are not always visible. Beginning at the southern end and heading north, you pass a variety of features from the area's natural and industrial heritage, including an impressive wall of sedimentary layers exposed by the Ventura River, active and abandoned industrial sites, the occasional oil derrick, and Highway 33. It may not be the most scenic stretch of trail you've experienced, but it is certainly interesting. The route is marked by a series of curious art installations that incorporate various themes related to Ventura. Installations include *A Delicate Balance,* bronze great egret and brown pelican sculptures; *Orange Trace,* clusters of painted bronze oranges arranged to look like they just fell from a freight car; and *Win*Pin,* a windmill/pinwheel hybrid sculpture that incorporates the poinsettia, Ventura's official flower.

By the time you reach the trail's midpoint, the pathway's scenery transitions slightly as it winds along pastureland and an equestrian path, with the Ventura River on one side and Ventura Avenue on the other. The trail is paved and in good condition, and crosses roads occasionally. Bicycle and pedestrian traffic on the trail is fairly light in the springtime, and picks up in the summer. Like most rail-trails, the Ventura River Trail is a very comfortable ride, though there is a slight uphill grade between the southern trailhead in Ventura and Foster Park. Foster Park is a lovely linear park along the Ventura River, and

Location
Ventura County

Endpoints
Main Street to Foster Park

Mileage
6

Roughness Index
1

Surface
Asphalt

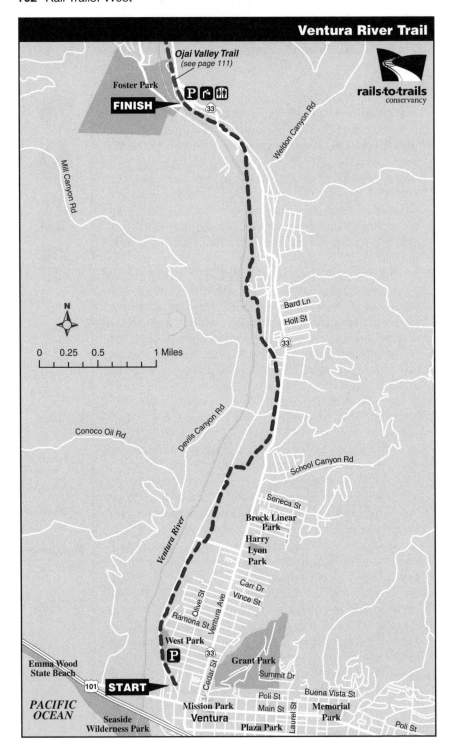

Ventura River Trail

Ojai Valley Trail
(see page 111)

Foster Park

P

FINISH

33

rails·to·trails
conservancy

Mill Canyon Rd

Weldon Canyon Rd

N

0   0.25   0.5   1 Miles

Bard Ln

Holt St

33

Conoco Oil Rd

Devils Canyon Rd

School Canyon Rd

Seneca St

Brock Linear Park

Harry Lyon Park

Ventura River

Carr Dr
Vince St

Olive St
Ventura Ave
Ramona St

West Park

P

33

Grant Park

Summit Dr

Emma Wood State Beach

101

START

Cedar St

Poli St
Main St
Buena Vista St
Laurel St

Memorial Park

PACIFIC OCEAN

Seaside Wilderness Park

Mission Park
Ventura

Plaza Park

Poli St

a popular spot for family barbeques on weekends. (It gets very busy on holidays!) The park has restrooms, water fountains and parking, which makes it a good starting point, though there is a $5 entrance fee.

If you're visiting Ventura for the first time, you may want to check out any of a number of interesting sites. Ventura's City Hall (the town is officially called San Buenaventura), a 1912 marble-and-terra cotta Beaux Arts building, provokes memories of a long-gone era of the Central Coast. The Ventura Pier, built in 1872, is Southern California's second-oldest pier and a great place to watch the local surfers catching waves.

DIRECTIONS

To reach the southern trailhead, exit Highway 101 onto Highway 33 North. Exit Highway 33 at Main Street, and head right (east). Make the first left (north) onto North Olive Street. Turn left again (west) onto Harriett Street. The trailhead is at the intersection of Harriett and Dubbers streets. Street parking is available nearby.

Contact: Parks Division
City of Ventura
501 Poli Street
Ventura, CA 93001
(805) 652-4550
www.cityofventura.net/parks_rec

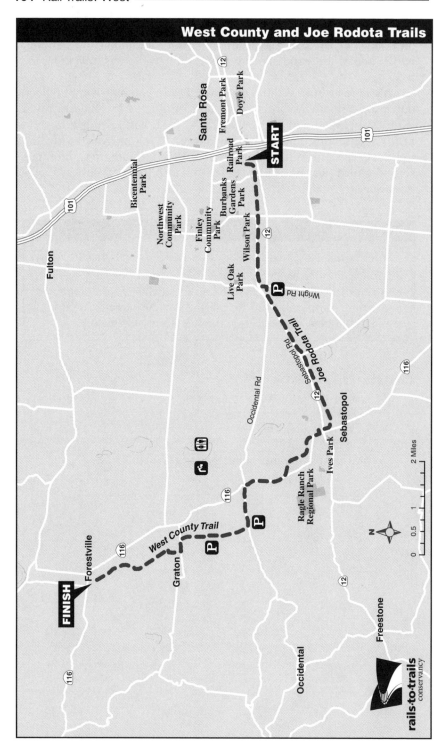

West County and Joe Rodota Trails

12

Santa Rosa

Fremont Park

Doyle Park

101

START

Railroad Park

Bicentennial Park

101

Burbanks Gardens Park

Finley Community Park

Northwest Community Park

Wilson Park

12

Fulton

Live Oak Park

P

Wright Rd

Sebastopol Rd

Joe Rodota Trail

Occidental Rd

12

Sebastopol

116

Ives Park

116

Ragle Ranch Regional Park

West County Trail

P

116

Forestville

Graton

P

FINISH

12

2 Miles

N

0   0.5   1   2

116

Freestone

Occidental

rails-to-trails conservancy

West County and Joe Rodota Trails

The West County and Joe Rodota trails take in some of Sonoma County's most scenic and sweeping rural vistas. The Joe Rodota Trail runs along the corridor of the old Petaluma and Santa Rosa Railway, which carried passengers among Santa Rosa, Petaluma and Sebastopol until it was abandoned in 1984. The rail-trail system was designated as a Community Millennium Trail by then-First Lady Hillary Clinton and the White House Millennium Council, in partnership with the U.S. Department of Transportation and Rails-to-Trails Conservancy.

The connection of the West County and Joe Rodota trails is an important recreation and commuting corridor that melds pastoral settings with community connections.

The Joe Rodota parking area and trailhead at Wright and Sebastopol roads in Sebastopol, close to the midpoint of the Joe Rodota Trail, is the recommended place to begin your trip. You could also go east toward Santa Rosa, traveling for just under 3 miles through an industrial area to the eastern endpoint at a creek in Roseland. The recommended and more scenic alternative, however, is to head west from the Wright Road parking area toward Sebastopol along Highway 12. This 3-mile westward section of the Joe Rodota Trail parallels Highway 12, and soon emerges into scenic farmland that evokes Sonoma County's pastoral heritage. The trail runs along a creek in places and you should be able to spot a variety of birds and wildlife as the trail meanders through the Laguna de Santa Rosa, the largest freshwater wetland complex in Sonoma County. If you're lucky, you may encouter a bald eagle, white pelican or osprey, all of which are known to inhabit this area.

Location
Sonoma County

Endpoints
Santa Rosa to Forestville

Mileage
13

Roughness Index
1

Surface
Asphalt

This straightaway section of the trail flows into Sebastopol and ends. To link to the West County Trail north of town, you have to cross the downtown area. As you enter Sebastopol, take a right on Petaluma Avenue. After a quarter mile, take a left on McKinley Street. Pass Whole Foods, then take an immediate right onto Main Street. Continue on Main Street for another quarter mile. Just before you reach the local high school, the trailhead will be on your left. The trail is wooded here and is a heavily used commuter route connecting the adjacent neighborhoods to the high school and downtown Sebastopol. After about a mile, the trail feeds into Gravenstein Highway. As you continue north along the highway you pass lush vineyards and farmlands before turning left onto Occidental Road. Stay on Occidental Road for just under another mile until you see the official signage on your right marking the trailhead for the original West County Trail.

This last 4-mile section of the trail passes through beautiful vineyards, picturesque farmland and orchards. A special treat is the fresh aroma coming from apple mills you pass on the second mile of the West County Trail. The trail ends at Ross Station Road in Forestville.

DIRECTIONS

To reach the trailhead at Wright and Sebastopol roads in Sebastopol, head north on Highway 101 toward Landfill Access Road just before reaching Santa Rosa. Take the State Highway 12 exit toward Sebastopol and merge onto Highway 12 West/Sebastopol Freeway. Turn left on North Wright Road, and immediately turn right at Sebastopol Road. The trailhead parking area will be on your left. Parking is also available in Sebastopol at the trailhead on Petaluma Avenue.

To reach the West County trailhead on Occidental Road, from Highway 101 take the Highway 12 West exit toward Sebastopol and continue for 3 miles. Turn right on Fulton Road and take an immediate left on Occidental Road. Follow Occidental Road for 5.2 miles until you see the West County trailhead parking area on your right.

Contact: Sonoma County Regional Parks Department
2300 County Center Drive, Suite 120A
Santa Rosa, CA 95403
(707) 565-2041
www.sonoma-county.org/parks/pk_westc.htm

West Side Rails: Hull Creek to Clavey River

If you're looking for quiet solidarity amid the beautiful, rugged scenery of the Sierra Nevada, this trail is for you. The Hull Creek segment of the West Side line is certainly off the beaten path, and you'll likely have the trail to yourself. Make sure you bring a good map and your sense of adventure, as finding the trailhead isn't easy and in places the railroad corridor itself isn't obvious even when you're on it. The trail is passable by mountain bicycle, but be prepared for a rough ride. You'll also need to carry your bike through the trail's several washouts and over fallen trees. The trail is great for hiking, but it's 8 miles one-way so make sure you come prepared and arrange for a pick-up.

For a great secluded hike or a challenging bike ride, try out the Hull Creek to Clavey River trail.

The trail begins near Hull Creek, in the heart of Stanislaus National Forest. As with the Sugar Pine Railway (page 143), interpretive signs about the railroad history are posted along the Hull Creek Trail. At the Mi-Wok Ranger District office in Mi-Wuk Village, you can pick up a brochure that corresponds to the tour signs. You will want to pick up two maps while you are there: one of the trail and another of the general area.

Park and begin at Signpost 2, site of Camp 24, which was once a busy hub for the railroad. At about 2.5 miles, you will reach Posts 4 and 5, which point out various relics from the railroad's past. Just beyond this point, the trail emerges into a meadow called Boney Flat. Post 11 marks the mile-long Trout Creek Spur, which climbs steeply then evens out as it approaches its endpoint at Forest Service Road 3N01 and Camp Clavey.

Location
Tuolumne County

Endpoints
Forest Service Road 3N86 to Camp Clavey

Mileage
8

Roughness Index
3

Surface
Ballast, dirt

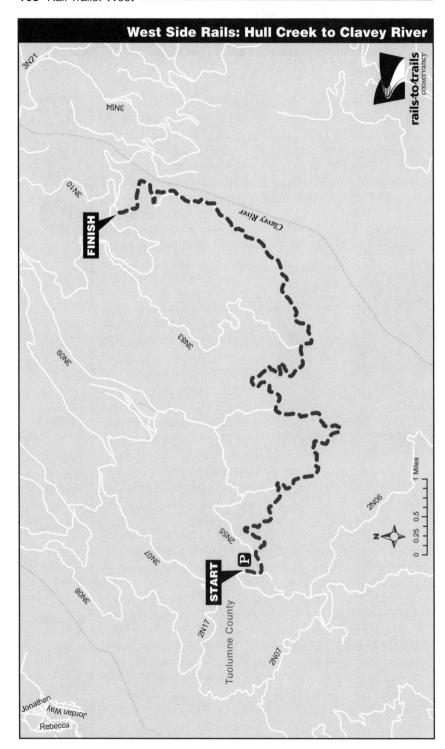

West Side Rails: Hull Creek to Clavey River

For more adventure, you can take a side trail to the old Clavey River Trestle before the trail leads you up toward Camp Clavey. At Post 11 near Buffalo Landing, head toward the river (right) on a side trail. A 75-foot trestle once stood here and burned down long ago. Its foundation remains though, standing as a testament to the rich railroad history of the Sierra Nevada.

DIRECTIONS

To reach the Hull Creek trailhead, from Highway 108 in Long Barn, turn east at the Merrell Springs turnoff, where there are signs for Hull Creek and Clavey River. Turn right (south) onto Long Barn Road and go 0.1 mile to Forest Service Road 3N01 (also known as 31 and North Fork Road). Follow FS 3N01, cross the North Fork of the Tuolumne River at 2 miles, then continue for 6.3 miles to Forest Service Road 3N07, where you will see a sign for the WEST SIDE RAIL TOUR.

Turn right (south) on Forest Service Road 3N07, continue for about 3 miles to an intersection. Stay on 3N07, which leads to a second road fork at 0.1 mile. Turn left (east) here onto Forest Service Road 3N86. The trail begins near the Hull Creek crossing, but it's best to continue another mile to Post 2 (the site of Camp 24), where several forest service roads intersect and there is more parking. The trail is Forest Service Road 3N86, and you can drive a vehicle on the road/trail until you reach Post 5 on the tour, although there is no parking there.

Contact: Mi-Wok Ranger District
Stanislaus National Forest
24695 Highway 108
Mi-Wuk Village, CA 95346
(209) 586-0262
www.fs.fed.us/r5/stanislaus/miwok

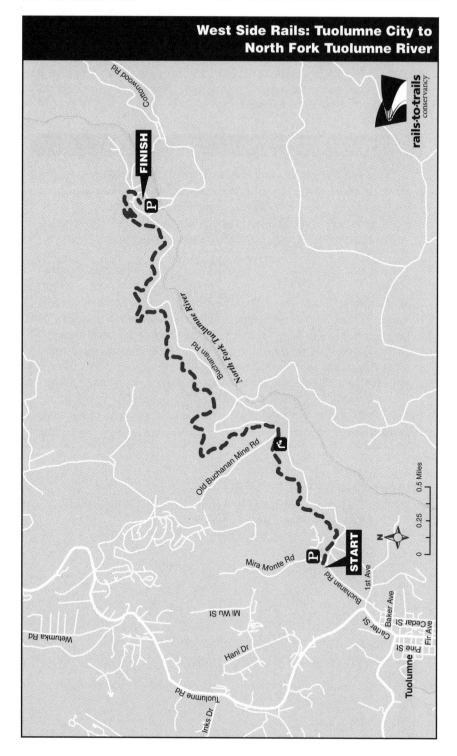

West Side Rails: Tuolumne City to North Fork Tuolumne River

West Side Rails: Tuolumne City to North Fork Tuolumne River

Tucked away in the sparsely populated Tuolumne County, this portion of the Stanislaus National Forest's West Side Rails is a hidden treasure, combining spectacular scenery and a route that represents an amazing feat of railway construction.

The timber industry was in full gear in the county at the turn of the century. An impressive sawmill was built at that time, and the West Side Lumber Company constructed its own Yosemite Valley Railway, to bring timber to the mill. In total, more than 70 miles of mainline track were constructed in the area. The initial stretch of the mainline grade, constructed without the benefit of bulldozers and loaders, was blasted into an extremely steep and rocky canyon. As you walk along this 5.5-mile rail-trail, you can't fail to be impressed by what the workers accomplished.

A hardy hiker is rewarded with dramatic views on the Tuolumne City to North Fork Tuolumne River trail.

Located next to a small parking lot and a residential street, the unsigned Tuolumne City trailhead is unassuming. As you start out you are surrounded on both sides by trees, but after less than a half mile the trail opens up to spectacular views. On your right you see a gaping canyon, with layers of rolling, tree-covered hills beyond. After another half mile, you come to a picnic bench and, shortly after, the only water fountain on the trail. (It's a good idea to bring water and protection from the sun.) At the 1-mile mark, you see the old rails and ties on the trail, which add to its beauty and character from this point on. The dramatic scenery continues as the path traverses the steep canyon. Patches of wildflowers that grow between the tracks appear in the springtime, making this rail-trail all the more beautiful.

Location
Tuolumne County

Endpoints
Buchanan and Mira Monte roads to Buchanan Road

Mileage
5.5

Roughness Index
3

Surface
Crushed stone, dirt

171

At certain points, the path becomes slightly narrow and rocky; if you are biking you probably will want to dismount unless you are comfortable riding on bumpier surfaces. At about 5 miles in, you will come upon a thick patch of trees that seems impassable, and you won't be able to continue walking parallel with the ties. From here you can return the way you came or veer right and descend the steep switchbacks for about 0.5 mile to a main road (Buchanan Road). Turn left here at the road and continue for a quarter mile to reach the River Ranch Campground. It is possible to leave a car here before setting out, and to then shuttle to the trailhead. If you're on a bicycle and want to return to the Tuolumne City trailhead parking lot via Buchanan, you can turn right and cycle for about 4.25 miles. The road is narrow at some points and steep, though, so use caution.

DIRECTIONS

To reach the Tuolumne City trailhead, from Highway 108, turn onto Tuolumne Road North. After approximately 7 miles, turn left from Tuolumne Road North onto Carter Street. Continue on Carter Street for less than 0.5 mile, then turn right onto Buchanan Road. After about 0.5 mile, you will see a small parking lot on the left at the intersection of Buchanan and Mira Monte roads. The trailhead is next to this parking lot.

To reach the Buchanan Road trailhead, continue on Buchanan Road past the parking lot for approximately 4.75 miles, and park at River Ranch Campground. From here, return the way you came for about 0.5 mile. The trailhead is on the right but is unmarked and easy to miss. Look for a gap in the canyon, and follow this path up the switchbacks to connect with the rail-trail.

Contact: Mi-Wok Ranger District
Stanislaus National Forest
24695 Highway 108
Mi-Wuk Village, CA 95346
(209) 586-3234
www.fs.fed.us/r5/stanislaus/miwok

Walk alongside a piece of California railroading history on West Side Rails: Tuolumne City to North Fork Tuolumne River trail.

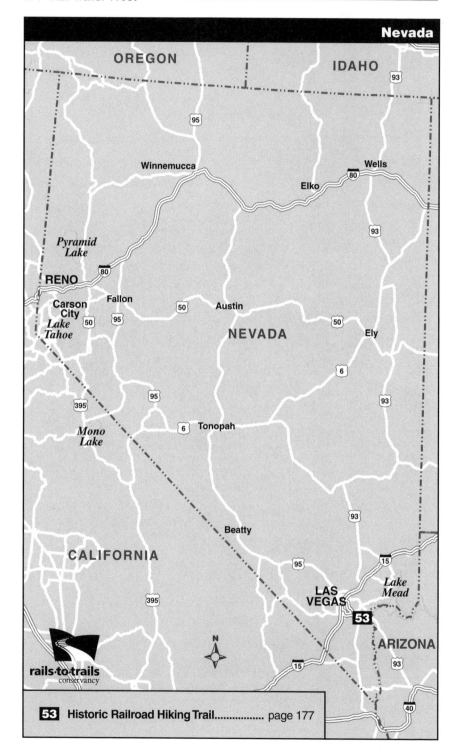

Nevada

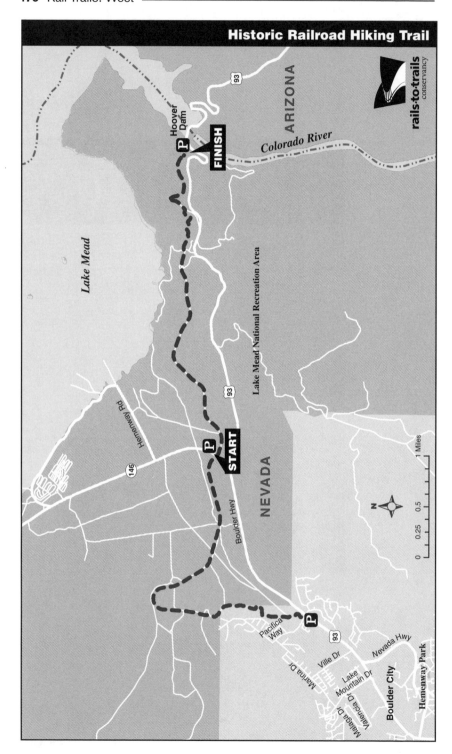

Historic Railroad Hiking Trail

ARIZONA

93

Hoover Dam

P

FINISH

Colorado River

Lake Mead

Lake Mead National Recreation Area

93

Hemenway Rd

P

START

146

NEVADA

Boulder Hwy

P

93

Pacifica Way

Ville Dr

Nevada Hwy

Martina Dr

Lake Mountain Dr

Malaga Dr

Valencia Dr

Boulder City

Hemenway Park

rails-to-trails
conservancy

N

0   0.25   0.5   1 Miles

Historic Railroad Hiking Trail

W hat happens in Vegas may stay in Vegas—but in the case of Nevada's Historic Railroad Hiking Trail, you'll want to tell everyone you know. Just 30 miles from Las Vegas outside Boulder City, the gravel rail-trail hugs the hills on the southern shoreline of vast Lake Mead. The trail offers panoramic views of the human-made lake and snakes through five railroad tunnels on its way toward Hoover Dam.

After the dam was completed in 1935, the railroad ceased operation, and in 1962 the tracks were removed. It wasn't until 1995, however, that the trail was opened for recreation. Though it begins obscurely at Highway 93 and Pacifica Way in Boulder City, the best place to begin your trek is the Lake Mead National Recreation Area Visitor Center (Alan Bible Visitor Center) trailhead at the trail's midpoint. Follow signs to pick up the trail at the edge of the parking lot and head southeast toward the lake. (Heading northward, you'll experience

The Historic Railroad Hiking Trail features five tunnels cut into the red rocky hillside to make a path for the rail line that hauled materials to the Hoover Dam construction site.

Location
Clark County

Endpoints
Highway 93 and
Pacifica Way to
Hoover Dam

Mileage
7

**Roughness
Index**
2

Surface
Gravel, dirt

Along most of its length, the trail is perched on a high hill with Lake Mead far below to the north and towering bluffs above you to the south.

3.6 miles of desert terrain trail through the Hemenway Valley, where jackrabbits bound over washed-out gullies, bighorn sheep graze, and the usual desert-dwelling snakes and lizards are at home.)

On the easy, wide path, you first pass through a high cut in the red, iron-rich, volcanic rock. The cut was blasted out in 1930 for trains to pass through, carrying stone to the dam site. As the trail curves toward the edge of Lake Mead, you'll find yourself several hundred feet above the grey-blue water. While the descent isn't a sheer drop, take care as there is no guardrail.

The lake views are spectacular all along the trail. Peaks of ancient volcanic mounds rise above the lake surface of this drowned valley like the humps of an aquatic beast. Far in the distance, the craggy, smoky blue South Virgin Mountains rise into the clouds.

Each of the five tunnels along the trail is 25 feet in diameter to accommodate the large equipment that passed through. In this unforgiving terrain, it's impressive to consider the sheer magnitude of force needed to blast the path. Pioneer trails from early dam construction parallel the trail intermittently.

Just before Tunnel 1, look down the ravine to the right to see concrete plugs taken from Hoover Dam to install turbines. You come across the first and second tunnels in quick succession, and their dark interiors provide a cool respite from the desert sun. (The Lake Mead National Recreation Area discourages hikers on any of its trails in the summer months, but fall and winter are prime touring seasons.) As you pass through Tunnel 2, notice that the ceiling and sidewalls have been reinforced. This work was done after the tunnel was burned as a result of arson in 1990. Wildfire gives rise to much of the plant life along the trail; creosote and mesquite bushes, which are fire-resistant, are scattered in green and brown bundles along the trail and on the surrounding hillsides.

In Tunnel 3 the arches were shored up to support the massive weight above. Fault lines are visible in the rippled texture of the sienna hillsides all along the trail, and particularly in the rock face about 20 feet before Tunnel 4. Passing through Tunnel 5, which was burned in 1978 and only reopened in 2001, you come to an opening in a fence where the trail continues.

Follow the trail as it snakes through some steep hillsides and industrial areas before reaching the endpoint in dramatic fashion; the trail brings you out on the top level of the visitor parking area, giving you an awe-inspiring view of the dam below. To reach the Hoover Dam Visitor Center, simply take the elevator down to the first level and follow signs. There is no question that this trail is an ideal way to visit the dam without battling the often heavy traffic on Highway 93.

DIRECTIONS

To reach the Boulder City Trailhead, from Las Vegas take Interstate 215 to Interstate 515 South. Follow I-515 South for 5.8 miles to Highway 93 toward Boulder City. After a little more than 8 miles on Highway 93, take a left onto Pacifica Way. The trailhead is immediately on the right.

To reach the Lake Mead Visitor Center Trailhead, from Las Vegas take I-215 to I-515 South. Follow I-515 South for 5.8 miles to Highway 93 toward Boulder City. After 9.6 miles take a left onto State Route 166. Look for the Lake Mead Visitor Center sign. Parking is available at the center. The trailhead is a little more than 0.3 mile ahead on the right.

Contact: Lake Mead National Recreation Area
601 Nevada Way
Boulder City, NV 89005
(702) 293-8990
www.nps.gov/lame/planyourvisit/hikerr.htm

STAFF PICKS

Popular Rail-Trails

When Rails-to-Trails Conservancy staff members traveled through the Western region to ride on, map and write about great rail-trails for this book, these were the ones that stood out as their favorites. Short or long, city or country, these are the rail-trails not to miss.

Arizona
Colorado River Trail
Peavine and Iron King Trails

California
Bayshore Bikeway
Bizz Johnson National Recreation Trail
Chandler Bikeway
Iron Horse Regional Trail
Lands End Trail
Mount Lowe Railroad Trail
Ojai Valley Trail
Old Railroad Grade
Sacramento River Trail (Redding)
San Clemente Pedestrian Beach Trail
Tiburon Historical Trail
West County and Joe Rodota Trails
West Side Rails: Tuolumne City
to North Fork Tuolumne River

Nevada
Historic Railroad Hiking Trail

ACKNOWLEDGMENTS

Each of the trails in *Rail-Trails: West* was visited by Rails-to-Trails Conservancy staff and volunteers. Maps, photographs, and trail descriptions are as accurate as possible thanks to the work of the following contributors:

Anne Zuparko

Barbara Brady

Ben Carter

Ben Gettleman

Cindy Dickerson

Eric Oberg

Frederick Schaedtler

Jason Barnes

Jen Kaleba

Joan Hackeling

Joel Gartland

Ken Bryan

Laura Cohen

Matt Hogan

Noel Keller

Phil Brady

Ryan Phillips

Sandy Simmons

Tim Rosner

INDEX

Become a member
of Rails-to-Trails Conservancy

As the nations's leader in helping communities transform unused railroad corridor into multiuse trails, Rails-to Trails Conservancy (RTC) depends on the support of its members and donors to create access to healthy outdoor experiences.

You can help support the future of rail-trails and enhance America's communities and countryside by becoming a member of Rails-to-Trails Conservancy today. Your donations will help support programs, projects and services that have helped put more than 15,000 rail-trail miles on the ground.

Every day, RTC provides vital technical assistance to communities throughout the country, advocates for trail-friendly policies at the local, state and national levels, promotes the benefits of rail-trails and defends rail-trail laws in the courts.

Join RTC in *"inspiring movement"* and receive the following benefits:

❶ New member welcome materials including *Destination Rail-Trails*, a sampler of some of the nation's finest trails

❷ A **subscription** to RTC's quarterly magazine, *Rails to Trails*.

❸ **Discounts** on publications, apparel and other merchandise including RTC's popular rail-trail guidebooks.

❹ The **satisfaction** of knowing that your dollars are helping to create a nationwide network of trails.

Membership benefits start at just $18, but additional contributions are gladly accepted.

Join online at **www.railstotrails.org**

Join by mail by sending your contribution to Rails-to-Trails Conservancy, Attention: Membership, 2121 Ward Court, NW, 5th Floor, Washington, DC 20037.

Join by phone by calling 1-866-202-9788.

Contributions to Rails-to-Trails Conservancy are tax deductible to the full extent of the law.